THE PHILOSOPHY OF THE PRESENT

PUBLISHED ON THE FOUNDATION
ESTABLISHED IN MEMORY OF
PAUL CARUS
EDITOR OF THE OPEN COURT AND THE MONIST
1888-1919

GEORGE HERBERT MEAD

THE PHILOSOPHY OF THE PRESENT

BY
GEORGE HERBERT MEAD

EDITED BY
ARTHUR E. MURPHY
Professor of Philosophy in Brown University

WITH PREFATORY REMARKS BY
JOHN DEWEY

Lectures upon the Paul Carus Foundation
THIRD SERIES

CHICAGO : LONDON
OPEN COURT PUBLISHING COMPANY
1932

PRINTED IN THE UNITED STATES OF AMERICA
FOR THE PUBLISHERS BY R. R. DONNELLEY
& SONS CO., CRAWFORDSVILLE, INDIANA

PREFACE

This volume contains the material from which Mr. Mead's *Philosophy of the Present* was to have been developed. No part of it, except the last two Supplementary Essays, was intended for publication in the form in which it now appears. Chapters One to Four are the Carus Lectures as read at the Meeting of the American Philosophical Association at Berkeley in December, 1930. They had not been planned as more than a partial statement of a more extensive project. Unfortunately, Mr. Mead, in his capacity as chairman of the department of philosophy at the University of Chicago, was forced to surrender the time he had set aside for the completion of the lectures to administrative concerns of an unexpected and disturbing character. As a consequence the lectures were written hurriedly, in large part on the journey from Chicago to Berkeley; and he had no opportunity in the weeks immediately following their delivery to begin the revisions he already had in mind. By the end of January he was seriously ill and he died within a few weeks. As here printed, the lectures are in substance precisely as they were presented at Berkeley; but the whole has undergone verbal revision, and the second lecture has been divided to form Chapters Two and Three. All footnotes are additions to the original manuscript.

After Mr. Mead's death there were found among his papers two additional manuscripts which are obviously preliminary drafts of the Carus Lectures. In large part these cover the same ground as the lectures themselves, but each also contains additional material of importance. The first three of the Supplementary Essays have been selected from these manuscripts. In the second, two parallel versions of the analysis have been retained. The difficulty of the exposition seemed to indicate the desirability of such repetition. The titles for these essays have been supplied by the editor. The fourth Essay is reprinted from the Proceedings of the Sixth International Congress of Philosophy, and the fifth from the International Journal of Ethics, April 1925. Each presents an essential aspect of Mr. Mead's theory not adequately dealt with in the lectures themselves.

Those who have known Mr. Mead through his teaching will feel keenly the incompleteness of this presentation of his philosophy. He himself was reconstructing his theory in the light of "emergent" material just as long as he was able to do so. At the time of my last conversation with him, in the week before his death, he was at work on Bergson's *Durée et Simultanéité* in its relation to his own account of relativity in Chapter Three. The importance of the material as it stands, however, both in the account it offers of the development of social experience and of scientific hypotheses, and in its suggestion of the more comprehensive theory toward which he was working seems fully to justify its publication in the only form in which it can now be made available.

I am greatly indebted to my colleague Professor Blake and to Miss Natalie Washburn for their generous help in the preparation of the manuscript for publication. The index is the work of Mr. F. K. Ballaine.

ARTHUR E. MURPHY.

Providence, R. I.
April, 1932.

CONTENTS

PAGE

INTRODUCTION xi

PREFATORY REMARKS xxxvi

CHAPTER

I THE PRESENT AS THE LOCUS OF REALITY 1

II EMERGENCE AND IDENTITY 32

III THE SOCIAL NATURE OF THE PRESENT 47

IV THE IMPLICATIONS OF THE SELF 68

SUPPLEMENTARY ESSAYS

I EMPIRICAL REALISM 93

II THE PHYSICAL THING 119

III SCIENTIFIC OBJECTS AND EXPERIENCE 140

IV THE OBJECTIVE REALITY OF PERSPECTIVES 161

V THE GENESIS OF THE SELF AND SOCIAL CONTROL . 176

INDEX 197

INTRODUCTION

The title Mr. Mead selected for these lectures—"The Philosophy of the Present"—contains an instructive ambiguity. The term "present" does not here refer directly to the contemporary situation in philosophy, but rather to the status of any object when it occurs and while it is occurring. If anything that exists is in some genuine sense temporal, as so many philosophers seem now to agree, then its foothold in reality is to be found in that present within which it not merely was or will be but effectively is, in the full and categorical sense. In a temporalist philosophy the tenses of the verb "to be" must be taken seriously, and Mr. Mead's theory is, above all things else, a philosophy of nature in the present tense. It seeks to understand the world as centered in a present, and to locate past and future, meanings and possibilities, in their function with respect to it. To see the past as past, for example, is to see it when it is past, in relation to the present whose past it is. What it, or anything else that claims existence, may be independent of its temporal reference, it is not empirically possible, and if Mr. Mead is right, it is not necessary, to inquire.

Yet the philosophy of being present is also, in a perfectly real sense, the philosophy of our contemporaries. "Process," "development" and "emergence" are catchwords of recent thought, and while the current is perhaps less strong to-day than it was ten or even five years ago it still represents a dominant theme among us. Mr. Mead's account will hardly take its place among the most popular manifestations of the "time spirit," but it does provide an unusually searching and independent analysis of its basic tendencies. Here is a temporalist philosophy that accepts its intellectual responsibilities. Those who "take time seriously" will find in it a thoroughly serious and consistently temporal standpoint from which to determine what "the philosophy of the present" in the present philosophical situation can contribute to a constructive and consistent theory of reality.

I

There are in this theory three related tendencies, each of which has its distinctive part in the total view. The setting of the problem and many of its characteristic developments are determined by a pragmatic theory of knowledge which Mr. Mead defended in his earlier works and which here, after brief restatement (pages 4-5), is accepted as a basis for what follows. Its influence is apparent (1) in the statement of the philosophic alternatives between which a choice must be made and (2) in the place given to "experience" as the ultimate referent of all knowledge claims.

(1) There are, for Mr. Mead, a whole set of traditional theories, all grounded in a false epistemology, which so interpret the objects to which knowledge refers as to place them "outside experience," not merely in the trivial sense that they are held to be other than the "immediate data of consciousness," but in the "metaphysical" sense of excluding from their permanent and self-contained reality the essential features of that world of common experience within which experiment and verification occur. When such objects are made the unique objectives of knowledge, experience, falling short of such reality, becomes "mere appearance," and the experimental validation that our ideas can in fact receive becomes irrelevant to the transcendent validity they are supposed to claim. In opposition to all such theories, pragmatists have held that knowledge is concerned not with any "antecedent" or "ulterior" reality, but

rather with the direction of activity in shared experience, and with objects in so far as they organize such activity around meaningful objectives of coöperative action. The reader will find, for example, in Mr. Mead's criticism of space-time as a "metaphysical" reality, that he has carried this familiar issue into the philosophy of science without essential modification of the basic dichotomy.

(2) Mr. Mead maintains that a view of this second type must defend its own ultimacy by holding that experience itself, as simply "there," "had" or possessed, has no ulterior reference—that there is no significant philosophical problem about the status of experience as such. And since consciousness, with its use of ideas and meanings, does involve such problematic reference, he further holds that consciousness is a development within experience, and not the final or inclusive form of our relation to it. This wider experience, the world which is "there" and with respect to which the problem of an external or transcendent reference does not arise, is foundational to Mr. Mead's view, and is assumed throughout.

Pragmatism as a philosophy has tended to encourage the activities of its protagonists in two directions. In many cases the polemical interest has been paramount, and here the sins and "pseudo-problems" of the epistemologist have come in for much attention. It seems not unjust to observe that while this criticism has played an important part in some earlier controversies it remains in itself too exclusively occupied with the very problems whose legitimacy it denies to offer great promise for the future. But when pragmatists have followed their enthusiasm for experience to the fact itself, and have called attention to the detailed structure of some objects of knowledge, their contributions have been outstanding. It was with this constructive pragmatism that Mr. Mead was primarily concerned. His approach to special problems of social psychology and of the history of scientific ideas was not at all that of a philosopher seeking ammunition for a special thesis; it was that of the painstaking, first-hand investigator, viewing the subject in its concrete detail and allowing it to tell its own story.

This second tendency in his thought is particularly manifest in his devotion to "research science" and to the objects and methods it presupposes. His insistence, against phenomenalism and relativism, that the material objects employed in physical experiment are neither to be reduced to sense-data nor dismissed as mere appearances is so emphatic as to call for defense against the suspicion that he is "hankering after the fleshpots of materialism." (page 148) It is not materialism but common sense, together with a healthy respect for the detailed process of physical discovery as opposed to sweeping generalizations, that governs his discussion of scientific objects in the third Supplementary Essay. And his own work in social psychology has its unique value as a contribution to the social sciences quite independently of any particular philosophic interpretation that may be placed upon it.

The third and perhaps the dominant strain in these lectures, however, is derived neither from pragmatism nor from research science, but forms part of that philosophy of nature which will no doubt be regarded as the characteristic contribution of the 1920's in Anglo-American philosophy. Alexander's *Space, Time and Deity* was the pioneer work in this transition from problems of knowledge—of "realism," "pragmatism" and "subjectivism"—to speculations about space and time and finally to metaphysics and the categories. The development of Whitehead's philosophy, from its early preoccupation with "sense data" and logical constructions, through the *Concept of Nature* with its "objects" and "events," to the daring speculations of *Proc-*

ess and Reality sums up in striking fashion the tendency of the period. And the principles of this development are natural enough. The various theories of knowledge that were phases of the "revolt against dualism" all sought to objectify those features of experience which a dualistic philosophy had regarded as merely subjective. This meant that what had previously been allocated to "mind" must now find its place in "nature" and that nature must be reconstructed accordingly. And finally, in the extension of relativity to the objective world, a criticism was required of the notions of "perspective," "time-system," "sociality" and the like, in order to show how these notions, purified of their merely subjective connotations, could take their place in a system of categories as the pervasive characters of reality. *The Philosophy of the Present* is an important contribution to this great undertaking.

To show that "social and psychological process is but an instance of what takes place in nature, if nature is an evolution" (pages 173-4) is the expressed intent of this later phase of Mr. Mead's philosophy. The principles of pragmatism are by no means abandoned, but they are generalized to include the whole process of evolution, and within this more general development distinctively human or conscious phases of "sociality" and relativity are to be understood as special cases of a process that takes all nature for its province.

Older problems recur here, but with a difference. The superficial reader may find in Chapter One only a revival of a too familiar controversy about our knowledge of the past. But in fact the theory is grounded not in special requirements of knowledge or verification but in what it means to be past and on the status of emergence and novelty in natural processes. The most original feature of these lectures is the daring extension of "the social" into what is at least a philosophy of nature, and, if the name did not offend a pragmatist, might also be called a metaphysic.

The pity is that Mr. Mead did not live to carry through the project which Chapters Three and Four serve at best to outline. Whether it could have been carried through consistently within the limits of a pragmatic theory of knowledge is a further question. My own view is that "sociality," like Whitehead's "feeling" is too essentially subjective a category for this metaphysic of process with which they were both concerned. But Mead, like Whitehead and Alexander, ventured as a pioneer into that territory of change and relativity which contemporary philosophy must certainly explore, and his chart of the country, incomplete as it necessarily is, may well prove of permanent value to those of us who follow, though less adventurously, the routes that have been opened for us.

II

The subject-matter of the lectures may be divided as follows. There is a theory about the nature of time and emergence, a theory about relativity and its social implications, and a synthesis of these in a theory of emergence as social and of sociality as a character of emergent evolution. In this section and the two following these topics are considered in this order.

The present is to be taken as the locus of reality. This means, I take it, that to consider anything as real is to consider it as existing in, or in relation to, a present. Now what, in relation to any present, is the status of its past? This is not to ask what it was when it was present, for then it was not past and did not stand in that relation by virtue of which it acquires the status of pastness. The past of an event is not just an antecedent present. This is Mr. Mead's main thesis throughout, but it does not often get as clearly expressed as in the following statement. "When one recalls his boyhood days he cannot get into them as he then was, without their relationship to what he has become; and if he could, that is, if he could reproduce the experience as it then took place, he could not use it, for this would involve his not being in the present within which that use must take place. A string of presents conceivably existing as presents would not constitute a past." (page 30)

The distinctive character of the past in its relation to the present is manifestly that of irrevocability. As conditioning the present, as making its occurrence possible, the past must have been of a determinate character. It expresses the settled condition to which the present must conform and without which it could not have been what it is. And this means not merely antecedent occurrence, it means causal determination or, as Mr. Mead tends to put it, the "carrying on of relations." The past is that out of which the present has arisen and irreversibility—the appeal might here have been made to Kant—has its critical value in terms of such conditioning.

Yet this carrying on of identical relations is never the whole story. The doctrine of emergence asks us to believe that the present is always in some sense novel, abrupt, something which is not completely determined by the past out of which it arose. A present, if it is really new at all, will have in it an element of temporal and causal discontinuity. Recent quantum physics has taught us to believe that such indetermination is quite consistent with rigorous physical analysis. (page 17) But how is it possible to reconcile this novelty with scientific determinism?

The answer to this question supplies the basic principles of the theory. Before the emergent has occurred, and at the moment of its occurrence, it does not follow from the past. That past relative to which it was novel cannot be made to contain it. But after it has occurred we endeavor to reconstruct experience in terms of it, we alter our interpretation and try to conceive a past from which the recalcitrant element does follow and thus to eliminate the discontinuous aspect of its present status. Its abruptness is then removed by a new standpoint, a new set of laws, from which the conditions of our new present can be understood. These laws could not have been a part of any previous past, for in the presents with relation to which those pasts existed there was no such emergent element. To assume a single determinate past to which every present must wholly conform is to deny emergence altogether. But at the same time, to treat the emergent as a permanently alien and irrational element is to leave it a sheer mystery. It can be rationalized after the fact, in a new present, and in the past of that present it follows from antecedent conditions, where previously it did not follow at all. As the condition of the present, the past, then, will vary as the present varies, and new pasts will "arise behind us" in the course of evolution as each present "marks out and in a sense selects what has made its own peculiarity possible." (page 23)

Is there any contradiction between this novelty of the past and its essential irrevocability? None at all, for the two apply in different senses. The irrevocable past is the past of any given present, that which accounts for its occurrence. Its determining conditions will be ideally if not actually fully determinable in the present to which it is relative. But when a new present has arisen, with emergent facts which were really not contained in the former present, its determining conditions, hence its past, will of necessity be different. The determinism then holds of the past implied in any present, the emergence in the relation of one such present, with its past, to another.

This hypothesis, in Mr. Mead's opinion, has two main

advantages. In the first place it accounts for the attitude of the research scientist toward the data he is describing, an attitude otherwise highly paradoxical. The laws of any science do in a sense reconstruct the past out of which its given elements have arisen. So much is assumed in the establishment of determinate laws, and for the scientist to suppose that the present did not follow from the past in terms of the laws he had established would be to deny their adequacy to the data they interpret. So far as it goes in any field science tends to be deterministic. Yet this "following" of present from past is wholly relative to the data on which the interpretation is based, and the scientist looks forward with equanimity to a new interpretation, and hence a new past, relative to the emergent data which the future will supply. And this combination of relative determinism and future reconstruction which holds for the research scientist, holds also, on this theory, for the nature he is describing.

Secondly, this view is in harmony with the emergence of novelty in experience, and the reorganization of experience in terms of it. This is the theme of the first Supplementary Essay. Even those who "bifurcate" nature most relentlessly must admit that in experience data may appear as intrusive elements in a world which has, in its present constitution, no place for them. They stand in contradiction to that world as currently interpreted and set a problem for reconstruction. To interpret the world exclusively in terms of the conditioning objects which a given period has isolated as the permanent background of becoming is to relegate novelty to a merely subjective experience. But in the case of data relevant to his own problems a scientist makes no such bifurcation. Rather does he treat the data as provisionally isolated in a world that does not now account for them, but as candidates for admission to a reconstituted world which may make the facts previously rejected the very center of its interpretation. So it was, for example, in the status of the Michelson-Morley experiment, first in its relation to classical mechanics, then in the theory of relativity. Within experience new objects are continually arising and a new present reorients the settled conditions of an older era in the light of its discoveries. And if the past is this orientation of settled conditions with respect to present data, the past does empirically change as evolution proceeds. This empirical description has been a part of Mr. Mead's philosophy for many years. The novelty of the present account arises from its correlation with the structure of temporal reality as such, in the relation of a determining past to an emergent present.

At this point the reader will be all too likely to object that it is clearly only our viewpoint or interpretation of the past that has altered here. The past in itself has surely not been changed by the new way in which we have come to look at it. This however is just the distinction that Mr. Mead's whole analysis attempts to supersede. For a temporalist philosophy the past "in itself" is not a past at all—its relation to the present is the ground of its pastness. And this relation is empirically a causal one. If becoming is real that causal relation is never such as to exclude emergence. When emergence occurs a new perspective of the past, a new relatedness, will ensue—a relatedness which is a natural fact about the new situation, though it could never have occurred in the old. And what is here new is precisely the way in which what, in the older present, was merely novel and abrupt has become a part of the world of causal objects, hence a part of the past through which they are supposed to operate. The relatedness is real, and the perspective past it generates, the past of the new present, is the real past of that present, and only for a present can the past be real at all.

Mr. Mead's most objective version of his thesis occurs in Chapter Two, in the contrast between the past as relative to a present and the past as absolute. He holds, especially in criticizing Alexander, that the past which physics requires is simply the expression of identical relations in nature, not an antecedent environment, existing in itself and giving rise, in its isolated being, to all subsequent reality. Space-Time in Alexander's metaphysic seems to be a mathematical structure taken out of relation to the physical data it interprets and transformed, in all its abstract independence, into a metaphysical matrix from which all the complexities of nature are somehow to be derived. This, on Mead's view, is just what the past "in itself" would be, a conditioning phase of natural process turned into a metaphysical substance. The search for such a substance is not ruled out for those whom it may concern. But the research scientist cares for none of these things.

We seem, then, to have discovered in temporal transition itself a unique sort of relativity, and a set of what we are now to describe as "temporal perspectives" or "systems." Each such system is distinguished by the temporal center from which its relation to past events is organized, and they differ primarily in this, that what is external, contingent, hence "emergent" for one such standpoint will "follow from" and hence be reflected in the past of another. How are such perspectives related, and how does the transition from one to another take place? The answer can be given only when we have inquired into the nature of relativity, and into its social implications.

III

The problem of relativity appears in its most crucial form, for Mead, in the theory of physical relativity. The

"Minkowski space-time" as even the most casual reader may gather, is his major preoccupation. The form of the problem is characteristic, and, whatever one may hold as to its solution, clearly raises an issue that philosophers who deal with this subject must face. What the theory of relativity has apparently done is to undermine the ultimacy, in scientific investigation, of the world of material objects in terms of which experimental physics has been accustomed to verify its theories. That world, as Mr. Mead argues in the first Supplementary Essay, is by no means a world of sense data or of private impressions. It is the world of solid macroscopic objects that can be measured and handled in common, objects whose permanent and relatively isolable characters can be identified under varying conditions, and mainly by the appeal from sight to touch, from distant to contact values, in what Mead calls the "manipulatory area." Lovejoy's devotion to the properties an object possesses "within its own spatio-temporal limits" furnishes eloquent testimony to the importance attached to such entities by common sense and its epistemological prophets. These are ultimate, standard properties in the sense that they provide the unquestioned criteria by which the dubious parts of experience can be tested. Of course, an epistemology that makes all experience a problem will find these factors as dubious as any, but the research scientist has not been much troubled by such considerations. His "materialism" has not been a godless metaphysics but rather an experimental reliance on contact values in measurement. If these, too, are "merely relative" and if they are valid only in reference to something else never in itself thus experimentally attainable, we seem to have placed our physical standard of validity clear outside the material world. A pragmatist can hardly fail to take account of such a crisis.

Now it seems to Mead that this is exactly what the

doctrine of space-time, taken in a simple and realistic sense, has done. It undermines the authority of the material object and its place in scientific experiment, without putting anything tangible in its place. This is evidenced in three ways. (a) The distinction between space and time is broken down. And for ordinary material objects this distinction is essential. "But from the standpoint of relativity no physical object can be isolated from what is happening to it." (page 144) There is no permanent character in it independent of its changes. Again (b) the values that attach to the newer physical object are not those which a material object can possess in itself, but are relative essentially. "Energy, like space-time, is a transformation value." (page 146) This means that the properties in terms of which we have previously identified our validating objects are variable, not constant, and "the metaphysical question is, can a thing with changing spatio-temporal and energy dimensions be the same thing with different dimensions, when we have seemingly only these dimensions by which to define the thing." (page 79) Now physics has often enough in the past relegated seemingly intrinsic characters to a merely relative status, but here the alteration is fundamental. For (c) it is no longer possible to interpret distance values in terms of possible contact experience or to regard the properties which a thing has *where it is* as uniquely characterizing it. The space and time values which an object has from a distance under conditions of relative motion will not be identical, even ideally, with those which a measurement of it in its own local space and time units would reveal. Nor can we simply correct the distance values, those given in terms of signals, by those which an observer at rest on the body itself would discover. For his calculations only come out even, when he imputes to us measured values which again would be falsified by experience in our manipulatory area, that is, with our local time and space standards. Thus, in the theory of relativity, distance experience, in terms of light signals, comes to have an autonomous value not reducible to contact or local values. This has been commented on with enthusiasm by Brunschvicg and with suspicion by Bergson, who reaches the conclusion that imputed times, those determined at a distance, do not really belong to their objects at all.

Mr. Mead reaches no such negative conclusion. He is content to follow the theory whither it leads and to accept space-time for whatever the scientist—as contrasted with the metaphysician—may find in it. Does this mean that we are to treat the measured values of physical objects as "subjective" and to set up—outside the experience in which we measure and manipulate—a new object standing in the same relation to primary qualities as that in which the primary have traditionally stood to the secondary? Space-time would then be a sort of attenuated material object without material properties. The alternative would be to reëxamine that whole relation of experience to its "real" or standard objects of which the problem about space-time is but an instance. Such reëxamination is Mr. Mead's contribution to the much argued subject of relativity. Its character can best be illustrated by examples drawn first from the familiar type of social interaction which is to serve as a model for the whole account, next from the physical field in which a scientific verification has normally operated and finally from the theory of relativity itself. In each case it is to be shown that the correction and organization of relative experiences in terms of the "real" objects to which they refer involves not a non-empirical reality to which they must somehow correspond, but rather a way of acting which relates past and future to the present from the standpoint or perspective of its widest social meaning.

There is a vast difference in ordinary social experience between what a man *has* and what he *owns*. Possession may be nine-tenths of the law but it is never the whole of it. Yet this further fact, additional to mere possession, cannot be embodied in a purely self-centered experience; it involves a reference to such claims as would be recognized in a court of law. The rights of property are objects of present experience in so far as any individual surveys his situation as an owner, in relation to the claims of others, and of the law, and reacts accordingly. To understand the implications of his conduct from this standpoint he must see them as others see them and must, in consequence, have come to take a socially objective attitude toward his own behavior. The meanings that this relationship confers upon experience are real and important facts about it. But they arise only for an individual who, as Mead would say, can react to his own reactions in the rôle of his fellows, and can take the standpoint thus achieved as authoritative for the direction of his own activity.

Thus to "take the rôle of the other" is to see all experience in a new context, in terms of what it means or portends relatively to the objects—or objectives—which this standpoint defines as central. The more of the past and future such a standpoint commands, the more will it transform experience into the substance of things hoped for and the evidence of things not seen and the more, above all, will it enlighten action by giving a present relevance and value to occurrences not literally given in immediate experience. The ordinary function of standard objects is to mediate action by bringing within the range of conscious selection alternatives that only this wider standpoint can encompass. The process of adjustment by which a child learns to play various parts in a social situation and finally to judge himself as a responsible person in the light of the value others would place upon his conduct, and which his own conscience, acting in their person, now accepts as authoritative, is outlined in the final Essay. It is the key to much that is most difficult, and most original, in the earlier Essays.

The second Essay attempts to extend this account of objectivity as "taking the rôle of the other" to our knowledge of physical objects. The requirements of the situation—if the analogy is to hold good—will be the following: (1) The meaning to be explained must be such as an individual experience could not possess in itself or in its immediacy; it must arise out of its interaction with external agencies. (2) It must nevertheless be possible for the individual to distinguish in experience between what is merely his own contribution and what on the other hand can be identified with the action of the other party to the transaction. If he is to react in the rôle of the other he must be able to identify some activity of his own through which and in terms of which he can act in its person. (3) The standpoint which he thus achieves must become so authoritative within experience that the meanings data take on in relation to it will be the index of their objective value. Finally (4) experience, as mediated by such meanings, will include the past and future, thus introducing into the present the conditions and consequences of the alternative reactions between which an individual must choose. To bring the conditions of action into the range of conscious deliberation in such fashion that we can direct conduct in the light of them is the goal of this whole development.

In our knowledge of physical things we can trace each of these factors. (1) The distinctive nature of the physical thing, its "having an inside," as Mead puts it, is not a character which our own experience, taken in its individual aspect, can reveal. We do not, for example, first discover an inside to our own bodies and then interpret others on this analogy. The body is known as a physical thing only in its relation to other physical things. "Genetically the infant advances from the periphery toward his body." (page 119) (2) It is the experience of resistance that provides the necessary external reference. In pushing and resisting things the organism can regard its own activity as identical in kind with that of the thing upon it. Action and reaction are equal and opposite. Thus in resisting the thing we are behaving towards it as it is behaving towards us. The "inside" of the physical thing, what it is for itself and in its own person, is thus what we find in contact experience, in the "manipulatory area." In the case of color, sound and the like there is no such persistent tendency to equate the thinghood of the thing with its effects in experience. (3) If we now assume that what experience would be from the standpoint of such a contact experience—what it is in its own spatio-temporal limits—is its real or standard nature we can judge its more immediate aspects accordingly. It is in leading up to the object as it exists where it is that distance experience becomes significant. We have here a standpoint, a relational focus of meanings, which, if we act in the rôle of the physical thing, becomes authoritative as against other perspectives or standpoints. "Real" shape and size, for example, are determined more correctly in the "manipulatory area" than they could be at a distance. There is some equivocation, I think, in Mr. Mead's use of the term "resistance" both for the deliverance of contact experience itself and also for the authority which such contact values come to have in directing or inhibiting our reactions to the thing. But his main view is clear. There are many contexts in which our experience is involved. The one we accept as a standard will determine the direction of activity and its meanings. It is by seeing the world as it would be for the fully realized values of thinghood that this standard is in fact applied. (4) The power of the human animal to discover such meanings transforms present experience into a world of objects whose potentialities are the possibilities of action. The scope of such action explains and justifies that transcendence of immediacy which epistemologists have so frequently emphasized and so rarely understood.

The application of all this to the theory of relativity is now comparatively easy, and the reader will follow it in Chapter Four and, in a less complicated statement, in Essay Four in fairly straightforward fashion. Again we have relative values, which, if Mead is right, are essentially social in the sense that they involve a reference, for their meaning, to that which exists outside the "time-system" within which they are reckoned. Again there is a search for something identical that will enable the individual to "take the rôle of the other" and to interpret experience not only from his own standpoint but from that, say, of the man on Mars. But here the range of the generalization has taken us clear beyond the physical object and its value of resistance. We are in the realm of a "generalized other," of an attitude which enables us to pass from any physical perspective to any other, occupying each—or any—in passage, and identifying in each only that which is in fact identical, the formula that justifies the transition from one to another. We have, then, in space-time, not a curious and unattainable new sort of object, but a generalization of that social objectivity which extends the generous capacity of seeing ourselves as others see us to include the views of our stellar neighbors. In this context of meaning the world of space-time has its locus and function. Nor does its importance discredit the physical object when the latter is viewed within its own proper limits. The conclusions of scientific research must not discredit the objects with which it operates and through which its conclusions are tested. But if space-time is understood not as the metaphysical superior of the physical object—the "reality" of which its relative being is but a "shadow"—but rather as a further development of that "community of interpretation" of which the physical object itself is a limited but highly valuable expression the two are perfectly compatible. We are then able to accept the theory of relativity as a phase—not necessarily final, of course—in that process by which man achieves social objectivity through the organization of relative perspectives.

IV

We are now ready for the most daring development in this theory. Can sociality—so far considered in its specifically human aspect—be so generalized as to characterize the whole course of natural development? We found relativity occurring in nature in the perspectives that emergence implies. And some sort of organization of such perspectives seemed to be required. If this readjustment should turn out—on all levels of development—to be a form of sociality, we should have succeeded in linking up sociality with the whole time process and putting mind back into nature with a vengeance. Thus "to present mind as an evolution in nature, in which culminates that sociality which is the principle and form of emergence" (page 85) is the final goal of the Carus Lectures. This culminating hypothesis took shape, if I can judge from my conversations with Mr. Mead, only while the lectures were being written. It remains the most suggestive and, as it stands, the most difficult part of his philosophy.

The sociality of emergence, and the evolution, through emergence, of sociality into higher and more complex objective expression are the parallel themes of this hypothesis.

(a) In what sense is emergence social? In emergence, as in the theory of relativity there is a plurality of "systems," that is to say of distinct standpoints, and we have the consequence that the "same" object must be in different systems at once. The system of physical relations is one thing, with its own organization of experience; the system of vital relations includes, as essential, elements which, from the merely physical standpoint, are external and contingent. And neither of these can be reduced to the other, since the vital really is emergent and hence additional to the merely physical while the physical is, in its scientific standpoint, determined exclusively by relations in which uniquely organic features of the world have no place. And yet the living animal belongs to both orders of relation and is in both "systems" at once. Consciousness is additional and irreducible to mere organic behavior, yet a sensation is at once an organic event and also implicated in that system of meanings which, in objectifying the possible future activity of the organism, is the distinctively conscious aspect of experience.

Sociality is "the situation in which the novel event is in both the old order and the new which its advent heralds. Sociality is the capacity for being several things at once." (page 49) But in its dynamic aspect it is more than this. The novel event must not merely be in two systems; it must adjust this plurality of systematic relations in such fashion that "its presence in the later system changes its character in the earlier system or systems to which it belongs" (page 69) while its older relations are reflected in the new system it has entered. It carries over the old relations, yet in its emergent novelty it reflects back upon the older world the uniqueness of its new situation. "So Rousseau had to find the sovereign and the subject in the citizen and Kant had to find both the giver of the moral law and the subject of the law in the rational being." (52) And so, to complete the picture, the monarchical system from which Rousseau's citizen and Kant's rational being emerged could never be quite the same again after their advent. The readjustment of the new social order to the old, of that which was carried over to that which emerged, is "sociality" in its most general sense. That it fits in neatly with the "reconstruction" of experience on the intrusion of novel elements as described in Section II will be evident.

The theory of relativity has been found consistent with "sociality" in its narrower sense. In Chapter Three Mr. Mead attempts to bring it under the more general formula he has now achieved. The "emergent" here will be that which appears only for some special perspective or "time-system" and is additional to that identical "carrying on of relations" expressed in the space-time structure common to the whole set of such perspectives. Motion is relative to the time-system selected, and the increase in mass which follows from increased velocity will occur only where the requisite motion occurs. And this "emergent" motion changes a physical character of the object—its mass—in that time-system within which it occurs. The analogy seems to Mr. Mead so obvious that he interprets more orthodox instances of "emergence" in terms of this one. "Emergent life changes the character of the world just as emergent velocities change the characters of masses." (page 65)

Now the body that moves in one time-system is as truly at rest in an alternative system—it is as much in the one as in the other. And its character in either is only adequately grasped when we understand its status in the other as well. Thus the relativist can explain the Fitzgerald contraction and its physical consequences only by assuming that the physically valid results reached in alternative time-systems will not in general coincide, and that each is to be seen therefore as relative, as requiring the recognition, as equally legitimate, of its alternatives. In this sense, that the physicist must be able to place himself in either perspective, the theory does indeed approximate the pervasive form of sociality as already outlined, and it is possible to refer to an increase in mass as "an extreme example of sociality." (page 52) To understand this increase as relative, as dependent on a special time-system and "emergent" for space-time as such, we must see the event in question both in the system in which the increase occurs and in that in which it does not and regard the event as genuinely a member of each.

When Mr. Mead goes beyond this to argue that the actual measurement of an increase in mass in one system requires the use, in this system, of space and time values derived from an alternative system (page 52 ff.) and hence that the two systems "cease to be alternatives" (page 54) the discussion becomes very involved and, if I have not misunderstood it, would seem to me mistaken. He could hardly, I think, have intended to retain it in its present form. But the main thesis is not necessarily compromised by the inadequacy of its detailed application. And the main thesis is this: The abruptness of emergent process is reflected in a plurality of relational systems irreducibly distinct yet so mutally implicated in "passage" that an object, belonging to two such "systems" at once will import into each a character with which its presence in the other has endowed it. The process of readjustment in which the object maintains itself in each system, through being also in the other, is sociality.

(b) How does sociality evolve? Since Mr. Mead holds that "the appearance of mind is only the culmination of that sociality which is found throughout the universe" (page 86) he naturally distinguishes between the common principle of this form of emergence and the special distinction it achieves in what is, so far as we know, its highest expression. With the common principle of sociality we are now familiar. The distinctive character of mind or consciousness is best seen in its contrast with the merely organic behavior from which it has emerged. "Primarily living forms react to external stimulation in such fashion as to preserve the living process. The peculiar method that distinguishes their reactions from the motions of inanimate objects is that of selection. This selection is the sensitivity of the living form. . . . The conscious animal carries selection into the field of its own responses. . . . Life becomes conscious at those points at which the organism's own responses enter into the objective field to which it reacts." (pages 71-3)

What it means to respond to one's own responses we have already seen. The relations in which the environment stands to our reactions are its meanings. To respond to such meanings, to treat them, rather than mere immediate data as the stimuli for behavior, is to have imported into the world as experienced the promise of the future and the lesson of the past. Meanings are now the very essence of what an object really is and in seeing it in terms of its meanings, in reacting to what it can do to us under crucial or standard conditions, we are bringing organic sensations into a new and emergent context. The human individual is alive and also conscious. His conscious behavior organizes his sensations—in themselves mere organic reactions—into qualities and meanings of things. This new place in a system of meanings alters the import of the sensation. Yet such behavior is dependent on the vital interactions from which it has emerged and the dependence of the thought on sensation carries over into the conscious system the reflection of its organic conditions. In reacting to the meaning of his sensations the individual is in both systems at once.

The highest level of conscious experience is, of course, that in which the individual can apprehend meanings in their fullest generality, and can thus command so wide a variety of standpoints toward his world as to isolate that which is common to all and would hence be valid for any rational individual. This is the rôle of the "generalized other," and the meanings which the sciences find in the world are those which so impersonal a standpoint will reveal. And yet it is just in this impersonality of standpoint that the individual becomes a "person"—a real member of the community of rational beings. To participate in the life of the community he must see himself as a participant and must respond to its claims and responsibilities as his own. In its person he can survey the "perspectives" which individual attitudes engender and can relate them all to the demands of the common purpose in which they are equally involved.

There is, clearly, a notable difference between that general "sociality" in terms of which an animal, by simply being both material and alive is "several things at once," with the resulting consequences of such systematic plurality, quite independently of any consciousness of the situation, and the more special situation in which an individual, by "taking the rôle of the other" can see himself from different standpoints and can make the correlation of these standpoints a part of the meaning of his world. If Mr. Mead has succeeded in portraying the latter situation as a natural "emergent" development from the former his major task is accomplished.

The argument returns at the end, as it should, to its point of departure. It is in a present that emergent sociality occurs. And we can now see that such a present is no mere moment of time, arbitrarily cut out from an otherwise uniform "passage of nature." A present is a unit of natural becoming; it is the period within which something temporally real can happen. What has been and what may be have their focus and actualization in a present standpoint and it is from such a standpoint that creative intelligence, transforming the novelty of emergence and the fatality of mere repetition into a measure at least of meaningful development, brings to articulate and self-conscious expression the pervasive form of natural process. It is as the scene of such process that the present is the locus of reality.

So original a hypothesis will naturally raise doubts and generate formidable problems. This, however, is not the place to consider them. The theory must speak first of all in its own person. In this introduction I have tried simply to "take the rôle of the other" and, interpreting the theory from its own standpoint, to bring together some of its main ideas, in such an order and relation as Mr. Mead might himself have adopted had he lived to complete the important work he had undertaken.

ARTHUR E. MURPHY.

PREFATORY REMARKS

The difficult task of drawing for the reader a map in which the main features of George Mead's thought are set before us (as is the business of a good map), in their proper relations to one another has been performed by Dr. Murphy in his Introduction. It would be of little or no assistance to the reader were I to go over the ground which he has traversed. There is, however, a trait of Mr. Mead's mind which when it is recognized will help protect the reader from some of the pitfalls into which one is likely to fall in dealing with an original thinker. While Mr. Mead was an original thinker, he had no sense of being original. Or if he had such a feeling he kept it under. Instead of bringing to the front as novelties the problems which were occupying his own mind (which they were even as problems), he chose to link them to ideas and movements already current. An excellent instance of this trait is found in the pragmatic theory of knowledge to which Professor Murphy refers. Mr. Mead does not seem to have had any consciousness of the way and the degree in which his own conception was a novel contribution; he preferred to treat it as if it were a natural outgrowth with at most some change of emphasis in statement.

When I first came to know Mr. Mead, well over forty years ago, the dominant problem in his mind concerned the nature of consciousness as personal and private. In the 'eighties and 'nineties, idealism prevailed in Anglo-American thought. It had a solution of the problem of consciousness ready to offer. Mind as consciousness was at once the very stuff of the universe and the structural forms of this stuff; human consciousness in its intimate and seemingly exclusively personal aspect was at most but a variant, faithful or errant, of the universal mind. I almost never heard Mr. Mead argue directly against this view. I suppose that it never seemed real to him in spite of the fact that it was the official doctrine of most of his own teachers and was, in some form or other, the philosophic conception most generally put forward in the philosophical writings of the period. When, however, it was urged upon him, instead of combating it, he took the ground that it did not touch the problem in which he was interested. Even if it were true and were accepted as such, it did not explain how states of mind peculiar to an individual, like the first hypotheses of a discoverer which throw into doubt beliefs previously entertained and which deny objectivity to things that have been universally accepted as real objects, can function as the sources of objects which instead of being private and personal, instead of being merely "subjective," belong to the common and objective universe.

As I look back I can see that a great deal of the seeming obscurity of Mr. Mead's expression was due to the fact that he saw something as a problem which had not presented itself at all to the other minds. There was no common language because there was no common object of reference. His problem did not fall into the categories and classifications of either idealism or realism. He was talking about something which the rest of us did not see. It lay outside of what used to be called "apperceptive masses." I fancy that if one had a sufficiently consecutive knowledge of Mr. Mead's intellectual biography during the intervening years, one could discover how practically all his inquiries and problems developed out of his original haunting question. His sense of the rôle of subjective consciousness in the reconstruction of objects as experienced and in the production of new customs and institutions was surely the thing which lead him to his extraordinarily broad and accurate knowledge of the historical development of the sciences—a knowledge which did not stop with details of discoveries but which included changes of underlying attitudes toward nature. His interest in the problem of self led in one direction to the study of the organism as the biological unit corresponding to the self. In the other direction it necessitated that study of the self in its social relations which carried him into social psychology—the field in which, I suppose, he had the greatest immediate influence through the effect of his teaching upon his students. The nature of his problem was such, as one can readily see, to make him acutely sensitive to the doctrines of Whitehead, especially the effort to include matters usually relegated to an exclusively subjective realm within the constitution of nature itself. Since his problem was (and that long before the words "emergent evolution" were heard), essentially that of the emergence of the new and its ultimate incorporation in a recognized and now old world, one can appreciate how much more fundamentally he took the doctrine of emergence than have most of those who have played with the idea. Against this background, his generalization of the idea of "sociality" and his interpretation of emergence in evolution take on a meaning which they do not otherwise have.

There is a passage to be found in the recently published first volume of Peirce's work which explains to me the kind of originality which marked Mr. Mead. "It is," Peirce said, "extremely difficult to bring our attention to elements of experience which are continually present. For we have nothing in experience with which to contrast them; and without contrast, they cannot excite our attention. . . . The result is that round-about devices have to be resorted to in order to enable us to perceive what stares us in the face with a glare that, once noticed, becomes almost oppressive with its insistency." The power of observing common elements, which are ignored just because they are common, characterized the mind of George Mead. It accounts for the difficulty which he had in conveying what he observed to others. Most philosophical thinking is done by means of following out the logical implications of concepts which seem central to a particular thinker, the deductions being reinforced by suitable concrete data. Mr. Mead's philosophical thinking often, perhaps usually, reverses the process. It springs from his own intimate experiences, from things deeply felt, rather than from things merely thought out by him, which then seek substantiation in accepted facts and current concepts. His interest in the concept of emergence is, for example, a reflex of that factor of his own intellectual experience by which new insights were constantly budding and having then to be joined to what he had thought previously, instead of merely displacing old ideas. He *felt* within himself both the emergence of the new and the inevitable continuity of the new with the old. So too he experienced within himself the struggle of ideas, hypotheses, presentiments, at first wholly private, a matter of intimate personal selfhood, to find and take their place in an objective, shared, public world. His sense of "sociality" as simultaneous existence in two different orders seems to me to have something in common with the combination of great originality and unusual deference to others which marked his own personality.

In contrast with the kind of originality which marked his thinking I realize that much which passes for original thinking is a reworking, in the light of some new perspective, of intellectual attitudes already pretty well conventionalized; the working of a vein of ore previously uncovered but not adequately exploited by others. I realize also that in much of what seems like clearness of literary expression, the clearness is but another name for familiarity rather than something intrinsic to the thought. The loss which American philosophy has suffered by Mr. Mead's untimely death is increased by the fact that there is every reason to think that he was beginning to get a command of his ideas which made communication to others easier and more effective. The manuscript of his Carus lectures—for whose careful editing we owe so much to Dr. Murphy—gives hardly more than hurriedly prepared notes of extreme condensation. He was planning to expand them to three or four times their present length, an expansion which would have clarified the thought and not merely swelled the number of words. But in spite of all limitations, I believe that a widening public will increasingly find in his writings what personal students have found for many, many years: a seminal mind of the very first order.

JOHN DEWEY

THE PHILOSOPHY OF THE PRESENT

CHAPTER I

The Present as the Locus of Reality

The subject of this lecture is found in the proposition that reality exists in a present. The present of course implies a past and a future, and to these both we deny existence. Whitehead's suggestion that, as specious presents vary in temporal spread, one present can be conceived which could take in the whole of temporal reality, would seemingly leave to us passage but would eliminate the past and the future. Whatever else it would be it would not be a present, for that out of which it had passed would not have ceased to exist, and that which is to exist would already be in that inclusive present. Whether this would still leave the character of passage might be doubted, but in any case the essential nature of the present and of existence would have disappeared. For that which marks a present is its becoming and its disappearing. While the flash of the meteor is passing in our own specious presents it is all there if only for a fraction of a minute. To extend this fraction of a minute into the whole process of which it is a fragment, giving to it the same solidarity of existence which the flash possesses in experience, would be to wipe out its nature as an event. Such a conspectus of existence would not be an eternal present, for it would not be a present at all. Nor would it be an existence. For a Parmenidean reality does not exist. Existence involves non-existence; it does take place. The world is a world of events.

There is little purpose or profit in setting up antinomies

and overthrowing the one by the other, or in relegating permanence to a subsistent, timeless world while the event, in which there is nothing but passage, is made the substantial element in existent things. The permanent character that we are interested in is one that abides in existence, and over against which change exists as well. There is, that is, the past which is expressed in irrevocability, though there has never been present in experience a past which has not changed with the passing generations. The pasts that we are involved in are both irrevocable and revocable. It is idle, at least for the purposes of experience, to have recourse to a "real" past within which we are making constant discoveries; for that past must be set over against a present within which the emergent appears, and the past, which must then be looked at from the standpoint of the emergent, becomes a different past. The emergent when it appears is always found to follow from the past, but before it appears it does not, by definition, follow from the past. It is idle to insist upon universal or eternal characters by which past events may be identified irrespective of any emergent, for these are either beyond our formulation or they become so empty that they serve no purpose in identification. The import of the infinite in ancient and modern mathematical thought illustrates this impotence.

The possibility remains of pushing the whole of real reality into a world of events in a Minkowski space-time that transcends our frames of reference, and the characters of events into a world of subsistent entities. How far such a conception of reality can be logically thought out I will not undertake to discuss. What seems to me of interest is the import which such a concept as that of irrevocability has in experience.

I will not spend time or rhetoric in presenting the moving picture of the histories that have succeeded each other from the myths of primitive ages up to Eddington's or Jeans' account of "The Universe about Us." It is only of interest to note that the rapidity with which these pasts succeed each other has steadily increased with the increase in critical exactitude in the study of the past. There is an entire absence of finality in such presentations. It is of course the implication of our research method that the historian in any field of science will be able to reconstruct what has been, as an authenticated account of the past. Yet we look forward with vivid interest to the reconstruction, in the world that will be, of the world that has been, for we realize that the world that will be cannot differ from the world that is without rewriting the past to which we now look back.

And yet the character of irrevocability is never lost. That which has happened is gone beyond recall and, whatever it was, its slipping into the past seems to take it beyond the influence of emergent events in our own conduct or in nature. It is the "what it was" that changes, and this seemingly empty title of irrevocability attaches to it whatever it may come to be. The importance of its being irrevocable attaches to the "what it was," and the "what it was" is what is not irrevocable. There is a finality that goes with the passing of every event. To every account of that event this finality is added, but the whole import of this finality belongs to the same world in experience to which this account belongs.

Now over against this evident incidence of finality to a present stands a customary assumption that the past that determines us is *there*. The truth is that the past is there, in its certainty or probability, in the same sense that the setting of our problems is there. I am proceeding upon the assumption that cognition, and thought as a part of the cognitive process, is reconstructive, because reconstruction is essential to the conduct of an intelligent being in the universe.[1] This is but part of the more general proposition that changes are going on in the universe, and that as a consequence of these changes the universe is becoming a different universe. Intelligence is but one aspect of this change. It is a change that is part of an ongoing living process that tends to maintain itself. What is peculiar to intelligence is that it is a change that involves a mutual reorganization, an adjustment in the organism and a reconstitution of the environment; for at its lowest terms any change in the organism carries with it a difference of sensitivity and response and a corresponding difference in the environment. It is within this process that so-called conscious intelligence arises, for consciousness is both the difference which arises in the environment because of its relation to the organism in its organic process of adjustment, and also the difference in the organism because of the change which has taken place in the environment. We refer to the first as meaning, and to the second as ideation. The reflection of the organism in the environment and the reflection of environment in the organism are essential phases in the maintenance of the life process that constitutes conscious intelligence.

I will consider the import of consciousness in a later lecture. At present my interest is only to locate that activity to which cognition belongs and of which thought is an expression. I am distinguishing in particular that existence of the world for the individual and social organism which answers to the more general usage of the term consciousness from that situation which answers to the term "consciousness of." It is the latter which, to my mind, connotes cognition. The distinction between the two falls in with that

---

[1] For a fuller account of this theory of knowledge see "A Pragmatic Theory of Truth," University of California Publications in Philosophy, Vol. 11, page 65 ff.

which I have suggested between the problem and its setting. The setting within which adjustment takes place is essential to the adjustment and falls within what belongs to the "field of consciousness," as that term is generally used—especially when we recognize the implications of that which is more definitely in the field of consciousness. The term "field of awareness" is at times used in the same sense, but it is more apt to carry with it the value of "awareness of" than is the term "consciousness." In other words, in knowledge there is always the presupposition of a world that is there and that provides the basis for the inferential and ideational process of cognition. This of course restricts cognition or "consciousness of" to that which has within it an inferential strain.

Now the world which is there in its relationship to the organism, and which sets the conditions for the adjustment of the organism and the consequent change in and of that world, includes its past. We approach every question of a historical character with a certain apparatus, which may be nicely defined, and this more technically defined material of documents, oral testimony, and historical remains subtends a given past which extends backward from the memories of yesterday and today, and which we do not question. We use the apparatus to answer hypothetically the historical questions which press upon us, and to test our hypotheses when they have been elaborated. It is of course understood that any part of this apparatus and of the past within which it is embedded may itself fall under doubt, but even the most heroic skepticism in its very enunciation cannot get away from the memory of the words and ideas which formulate the skeptical doctrine.

Some such given past is involved in questions bearing upon the past. And this given past extends the specious present. It is true that the ultimate agreement between the meanings of two documents may lie in experience in a specious present, but only upon the supposition of the comparison we have previously made of the documents. This comparison stretches back of us and remains unquestioned until someone points out an error therein and thus brings it into question, but then only upon the basis of his and others' past. Take the ingenious suggestion, of Gosse's father, I believe, that God had created the world with its fossils and other evidences of a distant past to try men's faith; and bring the suggestion up to a half an hour ago. Suppose that the world came into existence, with its exact present structure, including the so-called contents of our minds, thirty minutes ago, and that we had some ulterior evidence analogous to Mr. Gosse's fundamentalist views, that this had taken place. We could examine the hypothesis only in the light of some past that was there, however meager it had become. And this past extends indefinitely, there being nothing to stop it, since any moment of it, being represented, has its past, and so on.

What do we mean, now, by the statement that there has been some real past with all its events, in independence of any present, whose contents we are slowly and imperfectly deciphering? We come back of course to the very corrections which we make in our historical research, and to the higher degree of evidence of that which has been discovered over that which can be offered for the discarded account. Higher degrees of probability and added evidence imply that there is or has been some reality there which we are bringing to light. There is thus a palpable reference to the unquestioned past by means of whose evidence we investigate and solve the problems that arise. And the very fact to which I have referred, that any accepted account of the past, though not now in question, may be conceivably thrown into doubt, seems to imply some unquestionable past which would be the background for the solution of all conceivable problems. Let us admit this for the time being, and ask the further question whether this past independent of any present does enter at all into our investigations—I mean as a presupposition that plays any part in our thinking? If we should take away this presupposition would our apparatus and the operation of it in historical research be in any way affected? Certainly not, if we concern ourselves only with the problems with which historians in social or scientific history are concerned. Here the reference is always and solely to the given past out of which a problem has arisen; and the outlines of the problem and the tests to which presented hypotheses are subjected, are found in the given past. As we have seen, this given past may itself at a later date be affected with doubt and brought under discussion. And yet the possible dubiety of the given past in no way affects the undertaking. This is another way of saying that the dubiety of all possible pasts never enters into the historian's thinking. The only approach to such entrance is the demand that all past pasts should be accounted for and taken up into the latest statement. And every past past, in so far as it is reconstructed, is in so far shown to be incorrect. In the implications of our method we seem to approach a limiting statement, even if at infinity, which would fill out all gaps and correct all errors. But if we are making corrections there must seemingly be some account that is correct, and even if we contemplate an indefinite future of research science which will be engaged in the undertaking we never escape from this implication.

There is another way of saying this, and that is that our research work is that of discovery, and we can only discover what is there whether we discover it or not. I think however that this last statement is in error, if it is supposed to imply that there is or has been a past which is independent of all presents, for there may be and beyond doubt is in any present with its own past a vast deal which we do not discover, and yet this which we do or do not discover will take on different meaning and be different in its structure as an event when viewed from some later standpoint. Is there a similar error in the conception of correction of the past error and in the suggestion that it implies the absolutely correct, even if it never reaches it? I am referring to the "in-itself" correctness of an account of events, implied in a correction which a later historian makes. I think that the absolute correctness which lies back in the historian's mind would be found to be the complete presentation of the given past, if all its implications were worked out. If we could know everything implied in our memories, our documents and our monuments, and were able to control all this knowledge, the historian would assume that he had what was absolutely correct. But a historian of the time of Aristotle, extending thus his known past, would have reached a correct past which would be at utter variance with the known world of modern science, and there are only degrees of variance between such a comparison and those which changes due to research are bringing out in our pasts from year to year. If we are referring to any other "in-itself" correctness it must be either to that of a reality which by definition could never get into our experience, or to that of a goal at infinity in which the type of experience in which we find ourselves ceases. It is of course possible to assume that the experience within which we find ourselves is included in some world or experience that transcends it. My only point is that such an assumption plays no part in our judgments of the correctness of the past. We may have other reasons, theological or metaphysical, for assuming a real past that could be given in a presentation independent of any present, but that assumption does not enter into the postulations or technique of any sort of historical research.

While the conception of an "in-itself" irrevocable past is perhaps the common background of thinking, it is interesting to recur to the statement that I made earlier that the research scientist looks forward not only with equanimity but also with excited interest to the fundamental changes which later research will bring into the most exact determinations which we can make today. The picture which this offers is that of presents sliding into each other, each with a past which is referable to itself, each past taking up into itself those back of it, and in some degree reconstructing them from its own standpoint. The moment that we take these earlier presents as existences apart from the presentation of them as pasts they cease to have meaning to us and lose any value they may have in interpreting our own present and determining our futures. They may be located in the geometry of Minkowski space-time, but even under that assumption they can reach us only through our own frames of reference or perspectives; and the same would be true under the assumptions of any other metaphysics which located the reality of the past in pasts independent of any present.

It would probably be stated that the irrevocability of the past is located in such a metaphysical order, and that is the point which I wish to discuss. The historian does not doubt that something has happened. He is in doubt as to what has happened. He also proceeds upon the assumption that if he could have all the facts or data, he could determine what it was that happened. That is, his idea of irrevocability attaches, as I have already stated, to the "what" that has happened as well as to the passing of the event. But if there is emergence, the reflection of this into the past at once takes place. There is a new past, for from every new rise the landscape that stretches behind us becomes a different landscape. The analogy is faulty, because the heights are there, and the aspects of the landscapes which they reveal are also there and could be reconstructed from the present of the wayfarer if he had all the implications of his present before him; whereas the emergent is not there in advance, and by definition could not be brought within even the fullest presentation of the present. The metaphysical reality suggested by Eddington's phrase that our experience is an adventuring of the mind into the ordered geometry of space-time[2] would, however, correspond to a preëxistent landscape.

There is of course the alternative doctrine of Whitehead that perspectives exist in nature as intersecting time systems, thus yielding not only different presents but also different pasts that correspond to them. I cannot, however, see how Whitehead with the fixed geometry of space-time which he accepts can escape from a fixed order of events, even though the "what" of these events depends upon the ingression of eternal objects arising through the action of God, thus giving rise to emergence.[3] The point at issue is whether the necessity with which the scientist deals is one that determines the present out of a past which is independent of that or any present. An ordered space-time involves such a metaphysical necessity. From this standpoint the different pasts of experience are subjective reinterpretations, and the physicist is not interested in making them a part of the whole scheme of events. Whitehead's philosophy is a valiant attempt to harmonize this sort of geometric necessity with emergence and the differences of varying per-

[2] "Space, Time, and Gravitation," page 51.

[3] Mr. Mead's recurrent discussion of Whitehead is based mainly on "The Principles of Natural Knowledge" and "The Concept of Nature," with some reference also to "Science and the Modern World." He did not include "Process and Reality" in his discussion.

spectives. I do not believe that this can be accomplished, but I am more interested in the answer to the question, whether the necessity which is involved in the relations of the present and the past derives from such a metaphysical necessity, that is, from one that is independent of any present.

I revert here to my original proposition that a reality that transcends the present must exhibit itself in the present. This alternative is that found in the attitude of the research scientist, whether he confesses it in his doctrine or not. It is that there is and always will be a necessary relation of the past and the present but that the present in which the emergent appears accepts that which is novel as an essential part of the universe, and from that standpoint rewrites its past. The emergent then ceases to be an emergent and follows from the past which has replaced the former past. We speak of life and consciousness as emergents but our rationalistic natures will never be satisfied until we have conceived a universe within which they arise inevitably out of that which preceded them. We cannot make the emergent a part of the thought relation of past and present, and even when we have seemingly accepted it we push biochemistry and behavioristic psychology as far as we can in the effort to reduce emergence to a disappearing point. But granting the research scientist a complete victory—a wholly rationalized universe within which there is determined order—he will still look forward to the appearance of new problems that will emerge in new presents to be rationalized again with another past which will take up the old past harmoniously into itself.

Confessedly, the complete rationality of the universe is based upon an induction, and what the induction is based upon is a moot point in philosophic doctrine. Granted any justifiable reason for believing it, all our correlations greatly strengthen it. But is there such a reason? At this crucial point there is the greatest uncertainty. Evidently the scientist's procedure ignores this. It is not a moot question with him. It is not a question in his procedure at all. He is simply occupied in finding rational order and stretching this back, that he may previse the future. It is here that his given world functions. If he can fit his hypothesis into this world and if it anticipates that which occurs, it then becomes the account of what has happened. If it breaks down, another hypothesis replaces it and another past replaces that which the first hypothesis implied.

The long and short of it is that the past (or the meaningful structure of the past) is as hypothetical as the future. Jeans' account of what has been taking place inside of Aldebaran or Sirius Minor during the past millions of years is vastly more hypothetical than the astronomer's catalogue of what eclipses will take place during the next century and where they will be visible. And the metaphysical assumption that there has been a definite past of events neither adds to nor subtracts from the security of any hypothesis which illuminates our present. It does indeed offer the empty form into which we extend any hypothesis and develop its implications, but it has not even the fixity which Kant found in his forms of intuition. The paradoxes of relativity, what Whitehead terms the different meanings of time in different time systems, reveal the hypothetical nature of the ruled schedules of the past into which we are to fit the events which our physical theories unroll behind us. We may have recourse to the absolute space-time with its coincidences of events and intervals between them, but even here it is open to argument whether this interpretation of the transformations from one frame of reference to another is the final one, whether we have attained the ultimate structure of the physical universe or only a more powerful mathematical apparatus for reaching higher exactitude in measurements and calculations, whose interpretation will vary with the history of mathematical physics. The Minkowski space-time is as much an hypothesis as the de Broglie wave-constitution of matter.

But the irrevocability of the past event remains even if we are uncertain what the past event was. Even the reversible character of physical processes which mathematical equations seem to disclose does not shake this character of time experience. It may be thinkable that viewed from some vast distance the order of some of what we call the same events might differ in different perspectives, but within any perspective what has passed cannot recur. In that perspective what has happened has happened, and any theory that is presented must make room for that order in that perspective. There is an unalterable temporal direction in what is taking place and if we can attach other processes to this passage we can give to them as much of certainty as the degree of attachment justifies. Given a certain value for the velocity of a moving body in a certain frame of reference, we can determine where the body will necessarily be. Our problem is to determine just what it is that has preceded what is taking place so that the direction of temporal progress may determine what the world is going to be. There is a certain temporal process going on in experience. What has taken place issues in what is taking place, and in this passage what has occurred determines spatio-temporally what is passing into the future. So far then as we can determine the constants of motion we can follow that determination, and our analysis seeks to resolve the happening in so far as may be into motion. In general, since passage is itself given in experience, the direction of changes that are going on partly conditions what will take place. The event that has taken place and the direction of the process going on form the basis for the rational determination of the future. The irrevocable past and the occurring change are the two factors to which we tie up all our speculations in regard to the future. Probability is found in the character of the process which is going on in experience. Yet however eagerly we seek for such spatiotemporal structures as carry with them deducible results, we none the less recognize relations of things in their processes which can not be resolved into quantitative elements, and although as far as possible we correlate them with measurable characters we in any case recognize them as determining conditions of what is taking place. We look for their antecedents in the past and judge the future by the relation of this past to what is taking place. All of these relationships within the ongoing process are determining relations of what will be, though the specific form of that determination constitutes the scientific problem of any particular situation. The actuality of determination within the passage of direct experience is what Hume by his presuppositions and type of analysis eliminated from experience, and what gives such validity as it has to Kant's deduction of the categories.

It is the task of the philosophy of today to bring into congruence with each other this universality of determination which is the text of modern science, and the emergence of the novel which belongs not only to the experience of human social organisms, but is found also in a nature which science and the philosophy that has followed it have separated from human nature. The difficulty that immediately presents itself is that the emergent has no sooner appeared than we set about rationalizing it, that is, we undertake to show that it, or at least the conditions that determine its appearance, can be found in the past that lay behind it. Thus the earlier pasts out of which it emerged as something which did not involve it are taken up into a more comprehensive past that does lead up to it. Now what this amounts to is that whatever does happen, even the emergent, happens under determining conditions—especially, from the standpoint of the exact sciences, under spatio-temporal conditions which lead to deducible conclusions as to what will happen within certain limits, but also under determining conditions of a qualitative sort whose assurances lie within probability only—but that these conditions never determine completely the "what it is" that will happen. Water as distinct from combinations of oxygen and hydrogen may happen. Life and so-called consciousness may happen. And quanta may happen, though it may be argued that such happening stands on a different "level" from that of life and consciousness. When these emergents have appeared they become part of the determining conditions that occur in real presents, and we are particularly interested in presenting the past which in the situation before us conditioned the appearance of the emergent, and especially in so presenting it that we can lead up to new appearances of this object. We orient ourselves not with reference to the past which was a present within which the emergent appeared, but in such a restatement of the past as conditioning the future that we may control its reappearance. When life has appeared we can breed life, and given consciousness, we can control its appearance and its manifestations. Even the statement of the past within which the emergent appeared is inevitably made from the standpoint of a world within which the emergent is itself a conditioning as well as a conditioned factor.

We could not bring back these past presents simply as they occurred—if we are justified in using the expression—except as presents. An exhaustive presentation of them would amount only to reliving them. That is, one present slipping into another does not connote what is meant by a past. But even this statement implies that there were such presents slipping into each other, and whether we regard them from that standpoint or not we seem to imply their reality as such, as the structure within which the sort of past in which we are interested must lie, if it is an aspect of the real past. Passing by the ambiguities which such a statement carries within it, what I want to emphasize is that the irrevocability of the past does not issue from this conception of the past. For in our use of the term irrevocability we are pointing toward what must have been, and it is a structure and process in the present which is the source of this necessity. We certainly cannot go back to such a past and test our conjectures by actually inspecting its events in their happening. We test our conjectures about the past by the conditioning directions of the present and by later happenings in the future which must be of a certain sort if the past we have conceived was there. The force of irrevocability then is found in the extension of the necessity with which what has just happened conditions what is emerging in the future. What is more than this belongs to a metaphysical picture that takes no interest in the pasts which arise behind us.

In the analysis which I have undertaken we come then, *first,* to passage within which what is taking place conditions that which is arising. Everything that is taking place takes place under necessary conditions. *Second,* these conditions while necessary do not determine in its full reality that which emerges. We are getting interesting reflections of this situation from the scientist's criticism of his own methods of reaching exact determination of position and velocity and from the implications of quanta. What appears in this criticism is that while the scientist never abandons the conditioning of that which takes place by that which has gone on, expressed in probability, he finds himself quite able to think as emergent even those events which are subject to the most exact determination. I am not attempting to previse what later interpretation will be put upon the speculations of de Broglie, Schroeder, and Planck. I am simply indicating that even within the field of mathematical physics rigorous thinking does not necessarily imply that conditioning of the present by the past carries with it the complete determination of the present by the past.

Third, in passage the conditioning of that which is taking place by that which has taken place, of the present by the past, is *there.* The past in that sense is in the present; and, in what we call conscious experience, its presence is exhibited in memory, and in the historical apparatus which extends memory, as that part of the conditioning nature of passage which reflects itself into the experience of the organic individual. If all objects in a present are conditioned by the same characters in passage, their pasts are implicitly the same, but if, to follow out a suggestion taken from the speculations about quanta, one electron out of two thousand sets energy free, when there are no determining conditions for the selection of this electron over against the other nineteen hundred and ninety nine, it is evident that the past as exhibited in the conduct of this electron will be of a sort that will not even implicitly be the same as that of the others in that group, though its jump will be conditioned by all that has gone before. If of two thousand individuals under disintegrating social conditions one commits suicide where, so far as can be seen, one was as likely to succumb as another, his past has a peculiarly poignant nature which is absent from that of the others, though his committing of suicide is an expression of the past. The past is there conditioning the present and its passage into the future, but in the organization of tendencies embodied in one individual there may be an emergent which gives to these tendencies a structure which belongs only to the situation of that individual. The tendencies coming from past passage, and from the conditioning that is inherent in passage, become different influences when they have taken on this organized structure of tendencies. This would be as true of the balance of processes of disruption and of agglomeration in a star as in the adjustment to each other of a living form and its environment. The structural relationship in their reciprocal balance or adjustment arranges those passing processes which reflect backward and lead us to an account of the history of the star. As Dewey has maintained, events appear as histories which have a *dénouement*, and when an historical process is taking place the organization of the conditioning phases of the process is the novel element which is not predictable from the separate phases themselves, and which at once sets the scene for a past that leads to this outcome.[4] The organization of any individual thing carries with it the relation of this thing to processes that occurred before this organization set in. In this sense the past of that thing is "given" in the passing present of the thing, and our histories of things are elaborations of what is implicit in this situation. This "given" in passage is there and is the starting point for a cognitive structure of a past.

Fourth, this emergent character, being responsible for a relationship of passing processes, sets up a given past that is, so to speak, a perspective of the object within which this character appears. We can conceive of an object such as, say, some atom of hydrogen, which has remained what it is through immeasurable periods in complete adjustment to its surroundings, which has remained real in the slipping

[4] Cf. "Experience and Nature," chapters 3 and 7.

of one present into another, or, better, in one unbroken, uneventful passage. For such an object there would have been unbroken existence but no past, unless we should revert to the occasion on which it emerged as an atom of hydrogen. This amounts to saying that where being is existence but not becoming there is no past, and that the determination involved in passage is a condition of a past but not its realization. The relationship of passage involves distinguishable natures in events before past, present and future can arise, as extension is a relationship which involves distinguishable physical things before structurable space can arise. What renders one event distinguishable from another is a becoming which affects the inner nature of the event. It seems to me that the extreme mathematization of recent science in which the reality of motion is reduced to equations in which change disappears in an identity, and in which space and time disappear in a four dimensional continuum of indistinguishable events which is neither space nor time is a reflection of the treatment of time as passage without becoming.

What then is a present? Whitehead's definition would come back to the temporal spread of the passage of the events that make up a thing, a spread which is extended enough to make it possible for the thing to be what it is.[5] That of an atom of iron would not need to be longer than the period within which the revolution of each of its electrons around the nucleus is completed. The universe during this period would constitute a duration from the point of view of the atom. The specious present of a human individual would presumably be a period within which he could be himself. From the standpoint which I have suggested it would involve a becoming. There must be at least

[5] Cf. "The Principles of Natural Knowledge," 2nd ed., page 22 ff.

something that happens to and in the thing which affects the nature of the thing in order that one moment may be distinguishable from another, in order that there may be time. But there is in such a statement a conflict of principles of definition. From one standpoint we are seeking for what is essential to a present; from the other we are seeking for the lower limit in a process of division. I will refer to the latter first, for it involves the question of the relation of time to passage—to that within which time seems to lie and in terms of whose extension we place time and compare times. The thousandth part of a second has a real significance, and we can conceive of the universe as foundering in a sea of entropy within which all becoming has ceased. We are dealing here with an abstraction of the extension of mere passage from the time within which events happen because they become. In Whitehead's treatment this is called "extensive abstraction," and leads up to an event-particle as mathematical analysis leads up to the differential. And an event-particle should have the same relationship to something that becomes that the differential of a change such as an accelerating velocity has to the whole process. In so far, extensive abstraction is a method of analysis and integration and asks for no other justification than its success. But Whitehead uses it as a method of metaphysical abstraction and finds in the mere happening the event, the substance of that which becomes. He transfers the content of what becomes to a world of "eternal objects" having ingression into events under the control of a principle lying outside of their occurrence. While, then, the existence of what occurs is found in the present, the "what it is" that occurs does not arise out of happening, it happens to the event through the metaphysical process of ingression. This seems to me to be an improper use of abstraction, since it leads to a metaphysical separation of what is abstracted from the concrete reality from which the abstraction is made, instead of leaving it as a tool in the intellectual control of that reality. Bergson refers, I think, to the same improper use of abstraction, in another context, as the spatialization of time, contrasting the exclusive nature of such temporal moments with the interpenetration of the contents of "real" duration.

If, on the contrary, we recognize what becomes as the event which in its relation to other events gives structure to time, then the abstraction of passage from what is taking place is purely methodological. We carry our analysis as far as the control of subject matter requires, but always with the recognition that what is analysed out has its reality in the integration of what is taking place. That this is the result of defining the event as that which becomes, is evident, I think, in the application and testing of our most abstruse hypotheses. To be of value and to be accredited these must present new events springing out of old, such as the expansion or contraction of the universe in Einstein's and Weyl's speculations on the seeming recessions at enormous velocities of distant nebulae, or the stripping of electrons from atomic nuclei in the center of stellar bodies in Jeans' speculations upon the transformation of matter into radiation. And these happenings should so fit into our experimental findings that they may find their reality in the concretion of what is taking place in an actual present. The pasts which they spread back of us are as hypothetical as the future which they assist us in prevising. They become valid in interpreting nature in so far as they present a history of becomings in nature leading up to that which is becoming today, in so far as they bring out what fits into the pattern that is emerging from the roaring loom of time, not in so far as they erect metaphysical entities which are the tenuous obverse of mathematical apparatus.

If, in Bergson's phrase, "real duration" becomes time through the appearance of unique events which are distinguishable from each other through their qualitative nature, a something that is emergent in each event, then bare passage is a manner of arranging these events. But what is essential to this arrangement is that in each interval which is isolated it must be possible that something should become, that something unique should arise. We are subject to a psychological illusion if we assume that the rhythm of counting and the order which arises out of counting answer to a structure of passage itself, apart from the processes which fall into orders through the emergence of events. We never reach the interval itself between events, except in correlations between them and other situations within which we find congruence and replacement, something that can never take place in passage as such. We reach what may be called a functional equality of represented intervals within processes involving balance and rhythm, but on this basis to set up time as a quantity having an essential nature that allows of its being divided into equal portions of itself is an unwarranted use of abstraction. We can hypothetically reconstruct the past processes that are involved in what is going on as a basis for the cognitive construction of the future which is arising. What we are assured of by the experimental data is that we comprehend that which is going on sufficiently to predict what will take place, not that we have attained a correct picture of the past independent of any present, for we expect this picture to change as new events emerge. In this attitude we are relating in our anticipation presents that slip into others, and their pasts belong to them. They have to be reconstructed as they are taken up into a new present and as such they belong to that present, and no longer to the present out of which we have passed into the present present.

A present then, as contrasted with the abstraction of mere passage, is not a piece cut out anywhere from the temporal dimension of uniformly passing reality. Its chief reference is to the emergent event, that is, to the occurrence of something which is more than the processes that have led up to it and which by its change, continuance, or disappearance, adds to later passages a content they would not otherwise have possessed. The mark of passage without emergent events is its formulation in equations in which the so-called instances disappear in an identity, as Meyerson has pointed out.[6]

Given an emergent event, its relations to antecedent processes become conditions or causes. Such a situation is a present. It marks out and in a sense selects what has made its peculiarity possible. It creates with its uniqueness a past and a future. As soon as we view it, it becomes a history and a prophecy. Its own temporal diameter varies with the extent of the event. There may be a history of the physical universe as an appearance of a galaxy of galaxies. There is a history of every object that is unique. But there would be no such history of the physical universe until the galaxy appeared, and it would continue only so long as the galaxy maintained itself against disruptive and cohesive forces. If we ask what may be the temporal spread of the uniqueness which is responsible for a present the answer must be, in Whitehead's terms, that it is a period long enough to enable the object to be what it is. But the question is ambiguous for the term "temporal spread" implies a measure of time. The past as it appears with the present and future, is the relation of the emergent event to the situation out of which it arose, and it is the event that defines that situation. The continuance or disappearance

[6] "Identity and Reality" passim.

of that which arises is the present passing into the future. Past, present and future belong to a passage which attains temporal structure through the event, and they may be considered long or short as they are compared with other such passages. But as existing in nature, so far as such a statement has significance, the past and the future are the boundaries of what we term the present, and are determined by the conditioning relationships of the event to its situation.

The pasts and futures to which we refer extend beyond these contiguous relations in passage. We extend them out in memory and history, in anticipation and forecast. They are preëminently the field of ideation, and find their locus in what is called mind. While they are in the present, they refer to that which is not in that present, as is indicated by their relation to past and future. They refer beyond themselves and out of this reference arises their representational nature. They evidently belong to organisms, that is to emergent events whose nature involves the tendency to maintain themselves. In other words their situation involves adjustment looking toward a past, and selective sensitivity looking toward a future. What may be called the stuff out of which ideas arise are the attitudes of these organisms, habits when we look toward the past, and early adjustments within the act to the results of their responses when we look toward the future. So far these belong to what may be termed the immediate past and future.

This relation of the event to its situation, of the organism to its environment, with their mutual dependence, brings us to relativity, and to the perspectives in which this appears in experience. The nature of environment answers to the habits and selective attitudes of organisms, and the qualities that belong to the objects of the environment can only be expressed in terms of sensitivities of these organisms. And the same is true of ideas. The organism, through its habits and anticipatory attitudes, finds itself related to what extends beyond its immediate present. Those characters of things which in the activity of the organism refer to what lies beyond the present take on the value of that to which they refer. The field of mind, then, is the larger environment which the activity of the organism calls for but which transcends the present. What is present in the organism, however, is its own nascent activity, and that in itself and in the environment which sustains it, and there is present also its movement from the past and beyond the present. It belongs to the so-called conscious organism to complete this larger temporal environment by the use of characters found in the present. The mechanism by which the social mind accomplishes this I will discuss later; what I wish to bring out now is that the field of mind is the temporal extension of the environment of the organism, and that an idea resides in the organism because the organism is using that in itself which moves beyond its present to take the place of that toward which its own activity is tending. That in the organism which provides the occasion for mind is the activity which reaches beyond the present within which the organism exists.

But in such an account as this I have been implicitly setting up this larger period within which, say, an organism begins and completes its history as there seemingly in independence of any present, and it is my purpose to insist upon the opposite proposition that these larger periods can have no reality except as they exist in presents and that all their implications and values are there located. Of course this comes back, *first,* to the evident fact that all the apparatus of the past, memory images, historical monuments, fossil remains and the like are in some present, and, *second,* to that portion of the past which is there in passage in experience as determined by the emergent event. It comes back, *third,* to the necessary test of the formulation of the past in the rising events in experience. The past we are talking about lies with all its characters within that present.

There is, however, the assumed implication that this present refers to entities which have a reality independent of this and any other present, whose full detail, though of course beyond recall, is inevitably presumed. Now there is a confusion between such a metaphysical assumption and the evident fact that we are unable to reveal all that is involved in any present. Here we stand with Newton before a boundless sea and are only gathering the pebbles upon its shore. There is nothing transcendent about this powerlessness of our minds to exhaust any situation. Any advance which makes toward greater knowledge simply extends the horizon of experience, but all remains within conceivable experience. A greater mind than Newton's or Einstein's would reveal in experience, in the world that is there, structures and processes that we cannot find nor even adumbrate. Or take Bergson's conception of all our memories, or all occurrences in the form of images, crowding in upon us, and held back by a central nervous system. All of this is conceivable in a present whose whole richness should be at the disposal of that very present. This does not mean that the aeons revealed in those structures and processes, or the histories which those images connote would unroll themselves in a present as temporally extended as their formulation implies. It means, in so far as such an unbridled conception or imagination can have meaning, that we should have an inconceivable richness offered to our analysis in the approach to any problem arising in experience.

The past in passage is irrecoverable as well as irrevocable. It is producing all the reality that there is. The meaning of that which is, is illuminated and expanded in the face of the emergent in experience, like (a+b) to the 25th power by the binomial theorem, by the expansion of the passage which is going on. To say that the Declaration of Independence was signed on the 4th of July 1776 means that in the time system which we carry around with us and with the formulation of our political habits, this date comes out in our celebrations. Being what we are in the social and physical world that we inhabit we account for what takes place on this time schedule, but like railway time-tables it is always subject to change without notice. Christ was born four years before A.D.

Our reference is always to the structure of the present, and our test of the formulation we make is always that of successfully carrying out our calculations and observations in a rising future. If we say that something happened at such a date, whether we can ever specify it or not, we must mean that if in imagination we put ourselves back at the supposed date we should have had such an experience, but this is not what we are concerned with when we work out the history of the past. It is the import of what is going on in action or appreciation which requires illumination and direction, because of the constant appearance of the novel from whose standpoint our experience calls for a reconstruction which includes the past.

The best approach to this import is found in the world within which our problems arise. Its things are enduring things that are what they are because of the conditioning character of passage. Their past is in what they are. Such a past is not eventual. When we elaborate the history of a tree whose wood is found in the chairs in which we sit, all the way from the diatom to the oak but lately felled, this history revolves about the constant re-interpretation of facts that are continually arising; nor are these novel facts to be found simply in the impact of changing human experiences upon a world that is there. For, in the first place, human experiences are as much a part of this world as are any of its other characteristics, and the world is a different world because of these experiences. And, in the second place, in any history that we construct we are forced to recognize the shift in relationship between the conditioning passage and emergent event, in that part of the past which belongs to passage, even when this passage is not expanded in ideation.

The outcome of what I have said is that the estimate and import of all histories lies in the interpretation and control of the present; that as ideational structures they always arise from change, which is as essential a part of reality as the permanent, and from the problems which change entails; and that the metaphysical demand for a set of events which is unalterably there in an irrevocable past, to which these histories seek a constantly approaching agreement, comes back to motives other than those at work in the most exact scientific research.

Note to Chapter I [7]

Durations are a continual sliding of presents into each other. The present is a passage constituted by processes whose earlier phases determine in certain respects their later phases. Reality then is always in a present. When the present has passed it no longer is. The question arises whether the past arising in memory and in the projection of this still further backwards, refers to events which existed as such continuous presents passing into each other, or to that conditioning phase of the passing present which enables us to determine conduct with reference to the future which is

[7] These pages were found among Mr. Mead's papers after his death. They seem to have been written later than the chapter to which they are here appended, possibly as a result of a critical discussion of it at the University of Chicago Philosophy Club meeting in January 1931.

also arising in the present. It is this latter thesis which I am maintaining.

The implication of my position is that the past is such a construction that the reference that is found in it is not to events having a reality independent of the present which is the seat of reality, but rather to such an interpretation of the present in its conditioning passage as will enable intelligent conduct to proceed. It is of course evident that the materials out of which that past is constructed lie in the present. I refer to the memory images and the evidences by which we build up the past, and to the fact that any reinterpretation of the picture we form of the past will be found in a present, and will be judged by the logical and evidential characters which such data possess in a present. It is also evident that there is no appeal from these in their locus of a present to a real past which lies like a scroll behind us, and to which we may recur to check up on our constructions. We are not deciphering a manuscript whose passages can be made intelligible in themselves and left as secure presentations of that portion of what has gone before, to be supplemented by later final constructions of other passages. We are not contemplating an ultimate unchangeable past that may be spread behind us in its entirety subject to no further change. Our reconstructions of the past vary in their extensiveness, but they never contemplate the finality of their findings. They are always subject to conceivable reformulations, on the discovery of later evidence, and this reformulation may be complete. Even the most vivid of memory images may be in error. In a word our assurances concerning the past are never attained by a congruence between the constructed past and a real past independent of this construction, though we carry this attitude at the back of our heads, because we do bring our immediate hypothetical reconstructions to the test of the accepted past and adjudge them by their agreement with the accepted record; but this accepted past lies in a present and is subject, itself, to possible reconstruction.

Now it is possible to accept all this, with a full admission that no item in the accepted past is final, and yet to maintain that there remains a reference in our formulation of the past event to a something that happened which we can never expect to resuscitate in the content of reality, something that belonged to the event in the present within which it occurred. This amounts to saying that there is behind us a scroll of elapsed presents, to which our constructions of the past refer, though without the possibility of ever reaching it, and without the anticipation that our continual reconstructions will approach it with increasing exactness. And this brings me to the point at issue. Such a scroll, if attained, is not the account that our pasts desiderate. If we could bring back the present that has elapsed in the reality which belonged to it, it would not serve us. It would be that present and would lack just that character which we demand in the past, that is, that construction of the conditioning nature of now present passage which enables us to interpret what is arising in the future that belongs to this present. When one recalls his boyhood days he cannot get into them as he then was, without their relationship to what he has become; and if he could, that is if he could reproduce the experience as it then took place, he could not use it, for this would involve his not being in the present within which that use must take place. A string of presents conceivably existing as presents would never constitute a past. If then there is such a reference it is not to an entity which could fit into any past, and I cannot believe that the reference, in the past as experienced, is to a something which would not have the function or value that in our experience belongs to a past. We are not referring to a real past event which would not be the past event we are seeking. Another way of saying this is that our pasts are always mental in the same manner in which the futures that lie in our imaginations ahead of us are mental. They differ, apart from their successive positions, in that the determining conditions of interpretation and conduct are embodied in the past as that is found in the present, but they are subject to the same test of validity to which our hypothetical futures are subject. And the novelty of every future demands a novel past.

This, however, overlooks one important character of any past, and that is that no past which we can construct can be as adequate as the situation demands. There is always a reference to a past which cannot be reached, and one that is still consonant with the function and import of a past. It is always conceivable that the implications of the present should be carried further than we do actually carry them, and further than we can possibly carry them. There is always more knowledge which would be desirable for the solution of any problem confronting us but which we cannot attain. With the conceivable attainment of this knowledge we should undoubtedly construct a past truer to the present within which the implications of this past lie. And it is to this past that there is always a reference within every past which imperfectly presents itself to our investigation. If we had every possible document and every possible monument from the period of Julius Caesar we should unquestionably have a truer picture of the man and of what occurred in his life-time, but it would be a truth which belongs to this present, and a later present would reconstruct it from the standpoint of its own emergent nature. We can then conceive of a past which in any one present would be irrefragable. So far as that present was concerned it would be a final past, and if we consider the matter, I think that it is this past to which the reference lies in that which goes beyond the statement which the historian can give, and which we are apt to assume to be a past independent of the present.

CHAPTER II

Emergence and Identity

I have spoken of the present as the seat of reality because its character of a present sheds light upon the nature of reality. The past and the future that appear in the present may be regarded as merely the thresholds of a minute bit of an unbounded extension whose metaphysical reality reduces the present to a negligible element that approaches the world at an instant. This view of reality as an infinite scroll unrolling in snatches before our intermittent vision receives another variant in the picture of reality as a four-dimensional continuum of space-time, of events and intervals, forever determined by its own geometry, and into which we venture with our own subjective frames of reference, receiving momentary impressions whose present character is a function of our minds and not of any section of the ordered events in the universe. I have suggested that such an approach to reality does not answer to the scientific technique and method by which we seek for disclosures of the universe. Scientific procedure fastens upon that necessary conditioning of what takes place by what has taken place which follows from passage itself. In space-time relations, that is, in motion, this conditioning may reach the certainty of deduction, though even here we stand before the possibility that our conclusions may often rest upon statistical results which negate the final determination which we seek. There is evidence that the very effort to refine the technique to absolute precision defeats itself. Then there is the other branch of this determination of passage which we refer to under the caption of probability. Whatever our doctrine of probability, we assume that the happening of earlier events carries with it a probability as to the nature of later events, even if this probability can be reckoned only on a theory of chances. The basis of this determination of the future by the past is found in the fact that something is taking place which has a temporal spread—that reality cannot be reduced to instants—and that earlier stages must be conditions of later phases. It is the undertaking of science to find out what it is that is going on.

Furthermore the study of passage involves the discovery of events. These cannot be simply parts of passage. These events have always characters of uniqueness. Time can only arise through the ordering of passage by these unique events. The scientist finds such events in his observations and experiments. The relation of any event to the conditions under which it occurs is what we term causation. The relation of the event to its preceding conditions at once sets up a history, and the uniqueness of the event makes that history relative to that event. The conditioning passage and the appearance of the unique event then give rise to past and future as they appear in a present. All of the past is in the present as the conditioning nature of passage, and all the future arises out of the present as the unique events that transpire. To unravel this existent past in the present and on the basis of it to previse the future is the task of science. The method is that of ideation.

I have indicated that we find in the living form an individual thing that maintains itself through the mutual determination of the form and its environment. The surrounding world is so related to the animal or plant by their sensitivity and response that the life process continues. Over against the animal the world is one of food, shelter, protection or their opposites. Over against the inanimate thing the surroundings do not exhibit characters that answer to the action of the thing in being what it is. A boulder is a definite thing with its own mass and form, but its relations to things about it do not give rise to qualities in them which through the contacts, weight, or momentum of the boulder conserve the boulder. The boulder has no environment in the sense in which the animal has an environment. The background of the inanimate object is that of conservation—in our present day formulation, of the conservation of energy. No transformation affects the reality of the physical system. We have reduced matter and mass, in terms of which this presupposition was earlier formulated, to energy, but the essential feature of the doctrine has been that reality does not lie in the form—for there may be endless transformation—but in the matter, mass or energy. While, then, there has been a history of a stellar body, which may be traced in a causal series, science grasps the reality of the star only as it conceives of it as energy, which is unaffected whether the form of the body becomes a binary or a planetary system. The particular form of an inanimate body is irrelevant to "what it is." For such bodies the environment is as unessential as the object.

Plants and animals, however, present to science objects whose essential characters are found not in that which undergoes transformation but in the process itself and in the forms which the object assumes within that process. Since the process involves the interaction of animal or plant with surrounding objects, it is evident that the process of life as really confers characters upon the environment as it does upon the plant or the animal. However, plants and animals are physical objects as well as living objects. As physical objects their reality can be reduced to the whatever it is that is undergoing transformation, and their forms become unessential. As such they must be brought within the sweep of the physicist's and the chemist's doctrine. The life process is bound to disappear in the reduction of these processes to expressions of energy. The introduction of a vital force would help matters not at all; if it could be found it would inevitably be subject to the same reduction.

The difference between the physicist and the biologist evidently lies in the goals which their sciences contemplate, in the realities they are seeking. And their procedure answers to their goals. That of the physical scientist is reduction and that of the biologist is production. The biologist cannot investigate until he has got a life process going. He must, however, have physical means for this process and must therefore be a physicist as well as a biologist. If he reduces the reality of the life process to the means he is using he becomes a mechanist. If the life process appears to him a reality that has emerged out of the physical world, and his study is of the conditions under which it maintains itself, he is a teleologist. These two attitudes come into conflict with each other only if on the one hand he denies reality to the process because he can reduce to energy the objects that enter into it, and therefore refuses to recognize that the process that he is investigating is a reality that has arisen; or if, on the other hand, he states the physical and chemical things that enter into the process solely in terms of the process, and thus makes them Aristotelian qualities or adjectives. If he thus takes the position that all constituents of things are really potentialities of the thing which imply its pre-existence, then the biologist becomes an Aristotelian or, in a modern atmosphere, a "type" idealist; and, if he is consistent, surrenders the field of scientific research, and denies the possibility of emergence as well.

What I have wished to emphasize in this reference to the emergence of life is that it confers upon the world characters quite as genuine as those it confers upon living beings. This fact is recognized in the term environment. We are apt to use the term in a phenomenalistic fashion, to lodge the reality of the environment in its physical reduction to mass or energy, and to allow a real significance to the relation of the animal to his surroundings only in so far as these can be stated in physical and chemical terms. The reality of food, for example, is then found in the atoms or electrons and protons of which it is composed, and its nutritive character is a mere concession to our interest in an isolated group of happenings going on about us. As I have indicated, we cannot preserve this attitude without denying a fundamental reality to life. If life is a reality, its operation within form and environment must confer its characters within its whole field of operation. If an animal digests, there must exist a food which the animal digests. Another fashion in which to present the situation is in terms of the contrast between the conditions of that which takes place, and the conditioned occurrence. It has back of it also the distinction between things and events. The passing event solidifies into the thing as it becomes in the present the fixed conditions of later occurrences. Good digestion, health, and life itself are conditions for the varied activities which the future holds, and as such they are things that constitute some of our most precious possessions. They are, in especial, those contents to which varying characters or accidents are attached. In other words, they tend to become substances, being concreted by the fact that, having transpired, their conditioning nature, whatever it may be, is fixed. Thus the future is continually qualifying the past in the present.

The distinction which I indicated above between reduction and production falls in with that between our attitudes toward past and future respectively. The past we reduce to dependable conditions, and all the rich context of the future as it takes place, if it is to be comprehensible and serviceable, must be woven into this dependable web. Thus new things continually arise, the novelty of whose occurrence is worn down into the reliability of that which becomes familiar. But the thing is preëminently the physical thing of contact experience. We find here the fundamental relation between the future and the past in the present. The distance experience is the promise of contact experience. The something we can get hold of is the substance to which the qualities of sound, color, taste and odor belong. In the immediate perceptual world what we can handle is the reality to which what is seen and heard must be brought to the test, if we are to escape illusion and hallucination. The development of the distance receptors with their inner apparatus, the encephalon, has endowed the higher animals with a future which could become effective only in proportion as it was stretched out behind into the past in which the contact experiences that were promised or threatened by sight or sound were made specific by the finer adjustments of the hand in manipulation.

It was the peculiar advantage of Newtonian mechanics that its fundamental concept of mass was so closely correlated with the weight and volume of contact experience. It has always been easy for us to imagine the subdivision of perceptual objects into mass particles, and to translate inertia, force and momentum into the effort which contact experiences call out. In this mechanical doctrine the reliable conditions to which science has reduced the past have been made inherent in the mass particle, and the mass particle could be regarded as a refinement of the physical thing of the perceptual world. It is this peculiar agreement of the physical thing in science with the thing of perception that has given the so-called materialism of the doctrine its vogue. It is in no small degree to this correlation that we must attribute our instinctive tendency to ascribe the reality of life to the physical and chemical changes of inanimate things. The

Aristotelian found no difficulty in recognizing life as a nature that could belong to things, for he had no scientifically schooled imagination that could exhibit to him subperceptual physical things accomplishing living processes. Democritus offered this latter hypothesis, though without its experimental verification. I wish, however, to insist that the essential fallacy in this materialism, lies not in its assumption of a massive character for ultimate physical things—for mass has already disappeared in energy—but in the assumption that it is possible to give an exhaustive account of any event that takes place in terms of the conditions of its occurrence. I will not say that we cannot conceive of a passage within which nothing happens, but I do make bold to say that every event by which it becomes possible to differentiate passage must have a unique character which cannot be resolved into the conditions under which the event happens. The attempt so to resolve it leads not so much to materialism as to identical equations and a changeless Parmenidean block of reality. If this is true there is, of course, nothing peculiar in the emergence of life or of consciousness so-called. They may have had more import than other unique occurrences but other events have been as genuinely unique as they and have been as genuinely involved in the process of reality.

The striking feature in the appearance of life is that the process that constitutes the reality of a living being is one that extends beyond the form itself and involves for its expression the world within which this form lives. The reality of the process thus belongs to the world in its relation to the living being. This is referred to in the terms, form and environment. It is an expression of relativity in terms of life. The world is evidently a different affair for the plant and for the animal, and differs for different species of plants and animals. They have different environments. That we may reduce all of these to the physical world of the conditions under which life can go on, which is the field within which so-called purely physical processes take place, does not wipe out these various environments as aspects of reality.

The doctrine of relativity at present connotes a similar relation between any moving object or group of objects moving with the same velocity and in the same sense, and the rest of the world within which this consentient set[1] is moving. The spatial, temporal and energic characters of objects vary with the velocity of their motion in relation to the world that is at rest in respect to this moving consentient set. But, unlike the living form and its environment, the consentient set which is moving may be regarded as at rest, while its environment will then be regarded as moving with like velocity and in an opposite sense. The effect of relativity is then to carry what I have termed the reduction of physical science still farther; for if the same reality may appear indifferently as the motion of one set with reference to another at rest or as the motion of the second set with reference to the first, which is now at rest, it is evident that the temporal character of the objects at rest, their endurance or passage, must in some way be equated with the temporal character of the same objects in motion. The point-track of the first situation becomes equal to the translation in the second situation. We pass inevitably into a continuum in which time becomes a dimension. What was motion has become the interval between events in space-time, which, regarded from different standpoints, may be either rest or motion. A simpler if cruder way of saying this is that the reality of motion does not lie in the change but in the relative positions of things, regarded as events, with reference to each other.

[1] This term, with much of the exposition that follows, is borrowed from Whitehead, "Principles of Natural Knowledge," 2nd ed., chapter 3.

In the Newtonian world a boxlike space, conceivably filled with a stagnant ether, whose structure was irrelevant to time, was the absolute environment of all change, i. e., for the physical sciences, of all motion. The new absolute space-time is not the environment of anything for there is nothing going on there. There are only the events at intervals from each other. There is an ordered geometry of this continuum, and matter may be translated into this geometry in terms of curvature.

Something more has happened here than the disappearance of absolute space and time. These had already disappeared with the advent of a relational theory of space and time. It is no more possible to get evidence of an absolute motion from the standpoint of a relational theory than it is from the standpoint of relativity. What the Michelson-Morley experiment undertook to show was not the absolute motion of the earth through space, but its motion through the stagnant ether that was the accepted medium of light. But a new problem arose when Einstein proved that, by any system of measurement which could be instituted, the measurement of distances and times in a moving system from the standpoint of a system at rest would give a different result from that reached if the measurement took place within the moving system. The yardstick in the moving system would be shorter and the time measured would be longer. And this fell in with the transformations that Lorentz found necessary if Maxwell's electro-magnetic equations were to be rendered invariant. There was the same variation in the values of space, time and energy; and there appeared the constant value of light, which Einstein assumed for his measurement by signals. And this concurrent speculation by physicist and mathematician exactly accounted for the negative result of the Michelson-Morley experiment. On this new hypothesis, not only was it shown that evidence of an absolute motion was meaningless, but the process of measurement itself was shown, when it involved moving objects, to be highly complex, and to call for more complex mathematics and the genius of Einstein, who showed that the accepted results of Newtonian mathematics were but first approximations to more exact formulations. Thus the reduction of the conditions under which the measurements of exact science are made has been carried back of the structure of the space and time that had hitherto been presupposed. And the same is true of matter. The two attitudes with reference to matter which lie back of our perception and our thought are indicated in the two definitions which Newton gave of mass—as quantity of matter, and as the measure of inertia. The first is not capable of scientific use, since it presupposes determination of density; but it indicates a prevalent attitude of mind, the assumption of something that has a nature within itself, that can be grasped in independence of the relations into which it enters with other objects. Inertia can be grasped only through the relations of a body to other bodies. The attempt to define mass in terms of inertia leads to a circle—mass is defined in terms of force and force defined in terms of mass. It is necessary to presuppose a system in order to define the objects that make up the system. But the conception of a physical thing simply as that which occupies a certain volume, even if it did not provide a determinable quantity of matter, at least appeared to offer to the mind the objects out of which the system was to be built up. We meet the same conception in the hypothetical body Alpha which was suggested as located beyond the gravitational field, and as providing a fixed physical entity from the standpoint of which the physical universe could be oriented. If now we state the "what it is" of a body in terms of energy, we are implying a system as there in advance of the objects that make up the system. We have pushed our statement of the conditions which determine the nature of objects back of the perceptual object, and back of the subperceptual object of the Newtonian doctrine which merged so easily with perceptual experience. And we have lost the conception of an environment, such as that of the Newtonian space and Newtonian mass particles, within which the affairs of the physical universe can go on. For a space-time continuum does not provide such an environment. It is a metaphysical world of things in themselves, to which there may be a reference in the mathematical apparatus which we are obliged to use, but which does not provide us with an environment. It lacks the characters that are conferred upon an environment by an organism through its relationship to it, and has a nature out of which both organism and environment have arisen, and which may therefore be regarded as independent of them. The world of the physical and chemical sciences provides the conditions for life and the surroundings within which life may be lived. Evidently a world that lies beyond possible experience cannot be the environment of experience.

Nor can we regard two consentient sets moving with reference to each other as standing in the relation of form and environment, though the movement of one set confers upon the other a certain structure due to that movement. The fact that either set may be regarded as in motion, at least in so far as this change in structure is concerned, would make the conception of form and environment inappropriate. What we seek in the environment is a statement of the world out of which the emergent has arisen, and consequently the conditions under which the emergent must exist, even though this emergence has made a different world through its appearance. Newtonian matter in Newtonian space provided an original environment within which all changes took place, and Alexander presented space and time as such an environment out of which emerged matter, qualities, life, mind and deity. His philosophy was that of an emergent evolution, as the biologist Morgan presented it.[2] It had the historical sense which belonged to the period of evolution. Relativity does not belong to that period. Its more profound reductions of the exact conditions of existence open no doors toward the past. The early attempt to give it a metaphysical formulation eliminates change. It reduces time to a dimension on a parity with those of space, and substitutes geometry for history. Whitehead has indeed undertaken to preserve motion and change within a relativistic universe. He would keep the different time systems as perspectives in nature, but that he has avoided the rigidity of the geometry of the space-time continuum I cannot see, nor can I see how the ingression of eternal objects into events so determined can open the door to the contingent.

But it is not in these early metaphysical precipitates that I am interested. What does stand out from relativistic physical theory is that the reduction of the conditions of change, or in this case motion, has been carried so far back that change or motion itself disappears. Nor do we reach a situation out of which the change arises—except in so far as we set up a metaphysical realm which cannot be an environment within which the change takes place. On the contrary, space-time becomes a reality of which change is a subjective reflection. The same is true if we undertake to push back a theory of energy as the "what it is" of the physical object to the situations within which arise the objects which, as such, constitute the systems within which energy may be measured. Ostwald suggested such a doc-

[2] Cf. Alexander, "Space, Time, and Deity," Book III and Lloyd Morgan, "Emergent Evolution," chapter 1.

trine as this—that is, he set up energy as a metaphysical entity which does not as such come within the range of physical stuff,—an entity that can constitute an object in advance of the systems into which it can enter. Mass as quantity of matter offered such a conception, though it was not subject to exact definition. Still, it could be held in thought as the occupied volume, which exhibited itself in the resistance of inertia, and hence could be held in thought as a presupposition of the system of things. But an energy that can take various forms and still remain the same loses this empirical value. It can be presented in an object only in so far as a system of that type is already there. There must be an electro-magnetic system on hand to present an electron. To present a body whose content is so much energy in advance of the system is to posit a metaphysical realm which does not come within the range within which the scientist's hypotheses operate. This offers no difficulty as long as the hypotheses are occupied with the situations in which systems are already there. The "what it is" of the object can be defined in terms of the system. But the conception of energy as the nature of the physical thing does not provide us with an environment within which we can build up the system. Both the conceptions of relativity and of energy as the nature of the physical thing indicate that we have pushed our technique of exact measurement and our analysis beyond the point of historicity, i.e., we cannot go back to such a logical beginning as Alexander presented in his sweeping philosophy of emergence or evolution, or if we do we must reach it in some metaphysical realm which transcends scientific thought.

The striking fact is that these two phases of what I have called the reduction of the conditioning of passage—the conditions of measurement of that which is moving from the standpoint of that which is at rest—and the implications of accepting energy as the "what it is" of the physical object—I refer to the Larmor and Lorentz transformations as the conditions of the invariance of the Maxwell equations—should have come to the same conclusion at almost the same moment. The effect was to remove from the background of scientific thought an independent space and time within which a physical universe could be built up, and a matter which could be thought of in logical independence of the systems of things which were built up out of it. This background of historicity disappeared with relativity and the electro-magnetic theory of matter. For Newton space was the garment of God, and mass atoms were the preëxistent building stones out of which the world was constructed. The influence of such conceptions as an absolute space and mass particles led to the search for reality in causal series running back to ultimate entities that were the exactly measurable conditions of present reality. It was not at all necessary that such an implied absolute beginning should have been presupposed in determinate thought, but the concepts carried with them a set of mind that found reality in the conditions which, spread out, constitute the absolute past. The disappearance of an absolute space and the relegation of mass to a more general conception of energy emphasize *present* scientific findings as the test and seat of reality. Does the hypothesis of the preceding causal conditions fit into the data of observation and the laboratory? As long as it accomplishes this function its consonance with an ordered picture of a mechanical process is of no importance. Any hypothesis such as a wave theory of matter is welcome. Its test lies in its functioning. The set of the scientific mind toward its reality is away from the past and toward a present which carries within it the test of actual findings.

Yet we cannot desist from setting up histories; indeed

they become more fascinating. Compare for instance the excitement of Eddington's or Jeans' histories of stellar bodies with the monotony of a Newtonian mechanical structure or the Kantian or Laplacean hypotheses. But they carry with them no finality. We expect them to change with new problems and with new findings, and we should be greatly disappointed if they did not change. Nor do we expect them to become internally more consistent as in the case of the deciphering of an obscure manuscript. In scientific procedure there is no longer anything that conflicts with new pasts arising with emergent events.

CHAPTER III

The Social Nature of the Present

The social nature of the present arises out of its emergence. I am referring to the process of readjustment that emergence involves. Nature takes on new characters, for example with the appearance of life, or the stellar system takes on new characters with the loss of mass by the collapse of atoms through the processes that go on within a star. There is an adjustment to this new situation. The new objects enter into relationship with the old. The determining conditions of passage set the conditions under which they survive, and the old objects enter into new relations with what has arisen. I am here using the term "social" with reference not to the new system, but to the process of readjustment. An outstanding illustration is found in ecology. There is an answer in the community in the meadow or the forest to the entrance of any new form, if that form can survive. When the new form has established its citizenship the botanist can exhibit the mutual adjustments that have taken place. The world has become a different world because of the advent, but to identify sociality with this result is to identify it with system merely. It is rather the stage betwixt and between the old system and the new that I am referring to. If emergence is a feature of reality this phase of adjustment, which comes between the ordered universe before the emergent has arisen and that after it has come to terms with the newcomer, must be a feature also of reality. It can be illustrated in the appearance of a planet upon the hypothetical approach of the stellar visitor that occasioned the origin of our planetary system. There was a period at which the substance of our own earth was part of the sun's revolving outer sheath. Now it is a body separated from the stellar mass, still revolving, but in its own orbit. The fact that the planet is exhibiting the same momentum in its distant orbit as that which carried it about the star before its advent as a planet, does not do away with the fact that there is now a planetary system where here was formerly only a single stellar body, nor with that stage in which the substance of the planet to be was in both systems. Now what we are accustomed to call social is only a so-called consciousness of such a process, but the process is not identical with the consciousness of it, for that is an awareness of the situation. The social situation must be there if there is to be consciousness of it.

Now it is clear that such a social character can belong only to the moment at which emergence takes place, that is to a present. We may in ideation recall the process, but such a past is not a reintegration of the affair as it went on, for it is undertaken from the standpoint of the present emergence, and is frankly hypothetical. It is the past that our present calls for, and it is tested by its fitting into that situation. If, *per impossible,* we were to reach that past event as it took place we should have to be in that event, and then compare it with what we now present as its history. This is not only a contradiction in terms, but it also belies the function of the past in experience. This function is a continual reconstruction as a chronicle to serve the purposes of present interpretation. We seem to approach this complete recall, if I may use this expression, in identifying the fundamental laws of nature, such as those of motion, which we say must have been and must always be what they are now; and it is here that relativity is most illuminating. It frankly reduces the sort of reality that could be the identical content of past, present and future to an ordered arrangement of events in a space-time that, by definition, could be as little in any past of scientific imagination as it could be found in our perceptual world. The geometry of space-time denies emergence unless it is brought in by way of Whitehead's metaphysics; and if I am not mistaken such a view must surrender the ordered geometry of space-time that Whitehead retains. Without emergence there are no distinguishable events thanks to which time emerges. The events and intervals to which the relativist refers are the constants that shake out of the elaborate mathematics which the realization of the social character of the universe has shown to be necessary.

The social character of the universe we find in the situation in which the novel event is in both the old order and the new which its advent heralds. Sociality is the capacity of being several things at once. The animal traverses the ground in pursuit of his prey, and is at once a part of the system of distribution of energies which makes his locomotion possible and a part of the jungle system which is a part of the life system on the surface of the inanimate globe. Now we recognize that if we are to estimate the energy of locomotion that he is going to expend we must take into account his ferocity, his state of hunger and the attraction or fear that his prey excites within him, and equally we recognize that if we are to estimate these characteristics of the form we must be able to measure the energy-expressions in his organism and in the environment. There is as genuine a sociality in his relation to his environment as in his relation to the prey or to his mate or to his pack, and the mark of it is that we habitually estimate characteristics that belong to the object as a member of one system by those which belong to it in another. So we measure motion by the distances covered in the consentient set at rest, or the dimensions of that set by the motions involved in measurement. The relativist discovered that this mutual estimation involved a change in the units of measurement, and that a transformation must be made if ideal exactness is to be attained. We seem to be in the same situation in biology. Accurately to estimate the living process in energy-distributions we should be able to transform inorganic physico-chemical process into organic process, which unfortunately we have not been able to do.

If we examine the bases of this estimation from one system to another we find two characteristics, one is the emergence of the event from the conditions under which it has appeared—that which, as we have seen, gives rise to its history and may be brought under the general term of evolution. The second is the carrying on of identical conditions from the past into the present. The appearances of the planets, when related to the laws of mass and motion, fall into an ordered series, and from this standpoint the object is looked at as arising out of the old. From the standpoint of its emergence it is considered as in both systems, but only in so far common laws obtain in each. The substance of the arising planet is a piece of the sun, moving with the momentum which belongs to it in that capacity, and it is also an object in a system within which the sun has a definite mass that follows from the mass and motion of the planet with reference to the sun. In a similar fashion in Galilean dynamics accelerations and decelerations were emergents in a field of motion of masses in an absolute space.

It remained for relativity to set up motion itself as an entity which arises under certain conditions—those of frames of reference—out of logically antecedent conditions of events at intervals from each other within space-time. But these conditions no longer lie within the range of possible experience. It remains true however that what is motion from one standpoint within experience is rest from another. The relativity of motion had long been recognized. With the surrender of absolute space and the successful development of Einstein's general relativity, the emergence of motion and rest out of the more abstract situation that expresses what is common to both frames of reference or perspectives and appears in one as motion and in the other as rest, seems to be logically demanded. And yet, as I have just indicated, such a formulation takes us outside the scheme of development I have sketched above. It involves the relation of appearance and reality, of the subjective and the objectively real, not the relation of an emergent object arising out of the past to that which conditions it. We appear to have left an evolutionary philosophy of science and to be passing into a rationalistic phase in which reality is offered to us only in patterns of logic and mathematics. I suspect however that we are much too close to the great changes which have taken place within the last fifty years to be able to get them into their proper perspective.

I wish to suggest that the social character of the present offers another standpoint from which to regard this situation. I have spoken of the social implications of the emergent present as offered in the occupation by the new object of the old system and the new, sociality as given in immediate relation of the past and present. There is another aspect of sociality, that which is exhibited in the systematic character of the passing present. As we have seen, in the passage from the past into the future the present object is both the old and the new, and this holds for its relations to all other members of the system to which it belongs. Before the approach to our sun of the stellar visitor, the portion of the sun which became the earth was determined in its character by its relationships to those portions of the sun's substance which became the other planets. As it is drawn out into its planetary position it retains this character which arises from the former configuration and assumes the new character which is expressed in the perturbations of its orbit through the influences of its neighbors. The point is that a body belonging to a system, and having its nature determined by its relations to members of that system, when it passes into a new systematic order will carry over into its process of readjustment in the new system something of the nature of all members of the old. So in the history of a community, the members carry over from an old order their characters as determined by social relations into the readjustments of social change. The old system is found in each member and in a revolution becomes the structure upon which the new order is established. So Rousseau had to find both sovereign and subject in the citizen, and Kant had to find both the giver of the moral law and subject of the law in the rational being. To revert to the evolution of the planetary system, the earth's orbit still maps out the central sun of which it was a part, and its relative motions with reference to other members of the planetary system reflect their positions in the sun before the stellar visitor arrived.

I have referred to the increase in mass of a moving object as an extreme example of sociality. That is, if we keep this increase in mass within the field of possible experience, we have to treat the moving body as in two different systems, for the moving object has its own time and space and mass due to its motion, which time, space and mass are different from those of the system relative to which it is moving. The paradoxes arising out of this occupation of a different system on the part of a moving body are familiar. What I wish to point out is that we reach here the extreme limit of this sociality, for every body, thanks to its velocity, has a certain space-time and energy system. This velocity is, however, relative to the system within which the body is moving, and the body would have another velocity relative to another system moving with reference to the first. The body would then have an indefinite number of measurements of mass in the indefinite number of systems with reference to which it can be conceived of as moving. It is occupying all these different systems.

Now we may set up a metaphysical space-time, with its coincidences of events and its intervals, as the reality to which these frames of reference refer, or we may keep within the field of experience and use the transformation formulae which have been shown to be necessary for exact measurement. The question arises as to just what is involved in the use of the transformation formulae. In the immediate situations within which the relativity of motion is present in experience, such as the possibility of one's own train being in motion while the neighboring train is at rest, no transformation is required. In such cases we cover up the difference in time systems by saying that the differences in spatial and temporal dimensions are so impossibly small that they cannot be brought into application, that it is only when we reach velocities which approach that of light that appreciable differences arise and call for recognition. This is covering up a matter of fundamental importance. When a train is passing us it is in our own world of space and time. If we should take the relativistic standpoint and regard the train as at rest and the earth as rushing by it, we should indeed be passing from one perspective to another, but then the train would not be moving, and in the present case the train is moving. When we calculate the change in spatial, temporal and mass characters of an alpha particle which is shot out of an atom, we are treating it, of course, as in another space-time than our own, for we are giving to it the dimensions that belong to its space-time including the change in mass character. Now from the standpoint of Newtonian relativity two space-time systems are alternatives, they cannot both be applied to the same situation, except alternatively. But when we use the Lorentz transformation formula, we are giving the body the characteristics which belong to another space-time system and using the result in our own. This is confessed when the statement is simply made that a body increases its mass with its velocity, and we fail to add that the units of spatial and temporal measurement change also, that is, that we are in another frame of reference which is alternative to our own and cannot be simultaneously applied. We are told, however, that if an aeroplane were passing us at 161,000 miles a second we should see the foreshortening and the slowing down of the temporal extension of processes, that is, we should see in our own space-time system the effects of being in the other space-time system.[1] That is, the two frames of reference cease to be alternatives. In the case of the Fitzgerald foreshortening, there was no such assumption of being in both systems at once, but in this case there was no reference to difference in simultaneities.

Now Einstein undertakes to give the procedure by means of which we can be thus in one space-time system and record in it the effects of the differences due to the alternative space-time system. This procedure assumes first of all the uniform velocity of light as a fact in nature. In the second place on the basis of this uniform velocity of light a signal system is set up by which we can establish in our system that the same events are not simultaneous in the system that is moving with reference to ours as are simultaneous in our own. Furthermore, the effect of this difference can be made evident, as in the case of the passing aeroplane, through vision, that is, through light. What this amounts to is that as spatial perspectives arise for us in our static landscape, so there are discovered to be temporal perspectives over against moving

[1] Eddington, "Space, Time, and Gravitation," page 22 ff. For a more balanced account of the relativist theory the reader may consult A. Metz, "Temps, Espace, Relativité."

objects in the landscape. This perspective character of a temporal sort is discoverable only over against motions of very great velocities, but the principle of them is as definitely given as in the case of the spatial perspectives. That principle is that dimensions as revealed by measurement must be foreshortened in the direction of the motion, provided this takes place in a visual field. If the velocity of light were infinite there would be no foreshortening, for then the light wave that left one end of an object would reach us at the same moment as the light wave from the other end, no matter how rapid the motion. It is then only when velocities approach that of light that such a perspective enters into experience, and then only indirectly as in the calculation of the change in mass of the particle shot out of the atom. But if we could see what is found in Eddington's suppositious airplane we should get the visual temporal perspective directly, for of course time slows down in proportion as spatial dimensions are foreshortened. The natural assumption would be that these temporal perspectives are to be regarded in the same light as are spatial perspectives. The real dimensions and the real temporal passage are what the passengers in the airplane find them to be, just as their distorted view of us is to be corrected by what we find to be about us and what we find to be going on about us.

It is at this point that the Larmor-Lorentz transformations and the negative results of the Michelson-Morley experiment enter. These transformations were worked out to indicate the mathematically stated conditions under which the Maxwell equations for electro-magnetism would be invariant. The Newtonian equations are invariant within the field of Newtonian mechanics. That is, they hold whatever center of origin is taken as the center of reference and, in the case of the relative motion of systems with uniform velocity, whichever system is regarded as moving. It was found that to obtain invariance for the Maxwell equations it was necessary to affect the symbols referring to space, time and energy, including mass, with a coefficient 1/c in which c is the uniform velocity in a vacuum of the electro-magnetic wave, of which light is one form. The changes in spatial and temporal dimensions which this formula of transformation demands are those which the temporal perspectives, to which I have referred above, call for, and there is the same assumption of an absolute value for the velocity of light. Furthermore this transformation formula gives just the foreshortening of the earth's diameter in the direction of its motion in its orbit that accounts for the negative result of the Michelson-Morley experiment.

Apart from the striking coincidence in the results reached by means of the transformation formulae, Einstein's theory of relativity, and the result of the Michelson-Morley experiment, the outstanding fact is the common assumption of a constant velocity of light. In the case of the transformation formulae it is not surprising that the constant should be sought in so fundamental a character as the velocity of the electro-magnetic wave. In the case of relativity the possibility of measurement by light-signals in different time-space systems presupposes the uniformity of the velocity of light, and this is the explanation of the negative result in the Michelson-Morley experiment. "It means," I quote from Whitehead, "that waves or other influences advancing with velocity c as referred to the space of any consentient set of the Newtonian group will also advance with the same velocity c as referred to the space of any other such set."[2]

There should be added to the account of this conjunction the sweep of the atom out of the realm of mass mechanics into that of electro-magnetism, and the expression of energy-

---

[2] "Principles of Natural Knowledge," 2nd ed., page 43.

distribution in terms of fields. The importance of these changes lies in the change of reference of reality as between distance and contact experience. Formerly, there was a close correlation between mass mechanics and perceptual reality. The reality of what we saw was to be found in what we could get under our hands, and what we got under our hands accorded in imagination with mass as the quantity of matter. But the still more important point was that we felt the reality to lie in the volume itself in abstraction from its relations, that the reality of the thing could be there in advance of the system into which it entered. All the varieties of what I have called spatial perspectives of the same objects refer to identical objects found in the field of contact experience—of what we feel and see simultaneously—and this holds not only for our own perspectives but also for those of others. It finds its exact expression in congruence. What I have termed temporal perspectives do not occur in experience, except in such highly imaginative presentations as Eddington's airplane. But in perspectives which involve differences in simultaneities we seem to pass beyond the range of their perceptual resolution in the field of contact experience. We are compelled to bring them into accord by transformations. And this is just the situation which obtains in respect of the invariance of the Maxwell equations. The world from the standpoints of different space-time systems, with different values for the common units of space, time and energy, can only be assimilated by transformations. There is as close a parallelism between an electro-magnetic universe and the world of distance experience, that of visions, as between the world of mass mechanics and our contact experience.

However, there is a break in this complete correlation. As I have already indicated, the increase in mass of a moving body takes place in the space-time system within which it is moving, but the calculation of that increase in mass takes place by means of spatial and temporal units which belong to another space-time system, while the increase in mass is measured in the space-time system within which the motion is taking place. We actually find in measurement of our own pointer readings, with our own simultaneities, that the mass of the alpha particle has increased. We could discover that increase in mass without any use of the apparatus of relativity, but we account for it by a theory which implies that a clock on the alpha particle will be running slower than our clock, and it is by a calculation that involves the time of the alpha particle that we reach the change in mass which we discover in our own time system. In other words, the correlation breaks down at the point at which it is brought to the test of an experimental finding, which must have a reality of its own or it could not test the hypothesis. We must be able to state the facts involved in our own apparatus, clocks, electrometers in terms which are independent of the Lorentz transformations and the Einsteinian relativity. And in this world of final adjudication of the apparatus, the building that contains it and the ground on which it stands and its surroundings, the ultimate reality is not what belongs to distance experience, but to what can be presented in the contact experience which this distance experience promises or threatens. If we are not to go back of the field of experience into a metaphysical world of Minkowski space-time, with its events and intervals, we must come back to the perceptual world of scientific findings.

Let me state the situation again. The changes that take place in the field of electro-magnetism cannot be stated in a set of equations that are invariant for space and time. It is necessary to assume a different spatio-temporal structure in the field in which the change is going on. The clocks are going slower and diameters of things in the direction of the motion are decreased, while the mass is increased. These are changes which theoretically are all registered in the field which is at rest and within which the motion is taking place. But the calculation of them implies a spatio-temporal ordering which does not belong to that field. It implies another center of reference. The perceptual reality to which these changes in the field of distance experience refer differs according as they are taken from the standpoint of one field of reference or from another. This brings out the other striking character of the situation, that things whose substance belongs to the field of electro-magnetism cannot be defined in terms that allow of their being isolated as perceptual findings. For such definition it is necessary that a reality can be recognized in the thing that can be given in the spatio-temporal features of the perception—in pointer readings for example. This is the characteristic of mass, as I have insisted. Though we can define mass only in terms of a system of bodies in motion with reference to each other, we can think of the substance of the massive thing as found within the volume which we see or imagine, and can then put it actually or in imagination into relation with other things. Electricity as the substance of an electron can only be thought of in terms of its field and of the relations of that field with the fields of other electrons. Faraday's tubes of force and ether as a stuff have been used for the purpose of providing such an independent content, and have disappeared within our fingers. The fact is that science has come back to a structure of things that can be stated only in terms of distant experience so far as perception is concerned. This offers no difficulty in the structure of our theories. We know the amount of energy in a system and we can allocate it to the different members of that system, which can be located in space and time; but we cannot, so to speak, take a separate element in our fingers and say of it that this has a certain amount of energy within it which constitutes the "what it is" of the object, and then relate it to other things with like contents. Energy is conceivable only in terms of a system that is already there for the thought that deals with the thing. For the purposes of scientific method, the importance of contact experience does not lie in the greater reality of tactual or resistance experience over that of color or of sound, but in the fact that observation and experiment do come back to distance experience which must be itself directly or indirectly referred to what we can actually or conceivably get our hands upon. This remains the test of the reality of the perception, and is therefore the test of the scientist's finding in observation and experiment, and it is the condition of holding on to the fact as real in itself in independence of the varied hypotheses that are set up to account for it.

It has been customary to find the reality of the perception in the experience of the individual, and there have arisen all the multiform difficulties in placing this individual experience in the reality of the world to which he belongs, especially when such experience is used to criticize theories about that world. The scientist has been satisfied to find the same spatial and temporal structure in the individual's experience that he finds in the world, and thus to locate the individual's observations within the surrounding world, with all the exactness which spatio-temporal measurement makes possible. Now relativity, with the electro-magnetic theory out of which it has so largely arisen, has not only vastly complicated the spatio-temporal theory of measurement, but it has also reversed what I may call the reality-reference. Instead of saying that the reality of the perspectives of our distance experience is to be found in that contact experience which is firmly bedded in the geometry of a Euclidean space and the even flow of a uniform time, we must say that it is only as we can read over this seemingly Euclidean space of our contact world into perspectives dependent upon the motion of distance objects and discover transformation formulae between these that we can reach the reality of what we perceive. Furthermore we cannot proceed as we prefer to proceed, with perceptual models, and build up, say, a Bohr atom out of a number of protons and electrons welded into a nucleus around which we can set other electrons in planetary revolutions. The positive and negative electricity which we use as the stuff of these ultimate particles does not submit to such imaginative perceptual analysis. We may talk about the diameter of an electron or seek to locate its electrical charge, but the substantial character of electricity cannot be thus isolated, and the Bohr atom has broken down. In recent speculation it has been found convenient to deal with matter as a form of vibration, but there is no meaning in seeking for that which vibrates.

And yet the dependence of scientific theory upon perceptual findings was never more pronounced, and it is to this dependence that I would direct attention. As I have indicated the alternative seems to be a reference to a metaphysical world that can only be assumed, together with the assumption that the logical patterns which we find in our own world have correlates in this metaphysical world. In the meantime our experience becomes subjective except in so far as our thought relations may be guessed to transcend our frames of reference. In the prerelativity days the spatial and temporal structure of the observed fact was that of the universe. However relative to the observer the sense qualities of the observed object might be, its perceptual definition in space and time gave it fixed contour and location within the relational structure which for the scientist at least was the absolute structure of the world, and in mass mechanics the substantial content of any volume could be thought of as residing within that defined volume. Perception gave both the logical structure of reality and the defined habitat of substance. The earlier theory of gases and of heat as a form of motion is outstanding illustration of the simplicity of this situation. Now neither the relational structure of reality nor the locus of its substance is to be found in the perceptual situation. But since the scientist can never reach the metaphysical space-time with its events and intervals except by an assumption, and since he can never grasp the entire field of any energy content, he is obliged to test his hypotheses by placing himself both in his own perceptual situation of, say, a system at rest and also in that of the system which moves with reference to his own, and to compare the spatio-temporal structures of the two systems. He proceeds by transformations, but they are transformations which are possible only as the observer grasps that in his own situation which involves his placing himself in the situation of that which he observes. Although this is more complicated, it comes back in its findings to perceptual occasions. Now this is only possible if that sociality of thought in which we occupy the attitude of the other by taking our own divergent attitude is also a characteristic of nature. Newtonian relativity *permitted* the observer to transfer himself from one system to the other and to note that the relative positions of bodies in the two systems remained the same whichever system he occupied, and that the laws of mechanics were satisfied in either case. But electromagnetic relativity exhibits results within our system which *compel* us to have recourse to the other system with its space-time structure in order to account for them. Under Newtonian relativity sociality was confined to thought. Given the two systems moving with reference to each other, the conditions of either will forever remain the same, uninfluenced by the motion or rest of the other. Under electro-magnetic relativity the mass of the moving object increases in the system at rest, and this involves the different spatial and temporal coefficients of the other system. It is this break in what I have called the correlations between differences of space and time in different systems which reveals in the perceptual world that sociality in nature which has been generally confined to thought. The increased mass in the system at rest must also coincidentally be moving according to its own clock and in a space measured by its own yardstick, in order that there may be an increase in its mass within the other system. We have already seen that there is sociality in nature in so far as the emergence of novelty requires that objects be at once both in the old system and in that which arises with the new. Relativity reveals a situation within which the object must be contemporaneously in different systems to be what it is in either. The experimental proofs of relativity all come back to such situations.

I have pointed out that this is no novelty in science, though it has always implied an unsolved problem. We find it in teleology in biology and in consciousness in psychology. The animal species is in the mechanical system determined both by past conditions and also by tendencies to maintain itself in the future. The conduct of the conscious organism is determined both by a physiological system from behind and also by a consciousness which reaches into the future. This can of course take place only in a present in which both the conditioning past and the emergent future are to be found; but, as these problems indicate, what is further called for is the recognition that in the present the location of the object in one system places it in the others as well. It is this which I have called the sociality of the present. If we examine the situation from the standpoint of relativity, we see that the very motion that is taking place within the system at rest carries with it a different spatio-temporal structure, which is responsible for an increase of mass within the system at rest. If we translate this into the other two situations, we see a biochemical process arising which we call life, but which so changes the conditions under which it goes on that there arises in nature its environment; and we see living forms selecting those past conditions which lead to future maintenance of life and thus introducing values and later meanings into nature.

If we ask for the past that conditions the emergence of the present we can find no other formulation for it than this, that whatever emerges must be subject to the conditioning character of the present, and that it must be possible to state the emergent in terms of the conditioning past. In Newtonian relativity, in the case of unaccelerated motion of two systems with reference to each other, the conditioning past was summed up in the dictum of the same relative position of the bodies of the two systems and the same mechanical situation whichever system was regarded as in motion. In this situation there is no emergence. If into this Newtonian relativity we now introduce the Special Principle of relativity we have the emergence of new characters of the moving body in the system within which it moves, because of its motion. And if we describe the body under the old conditions we must reduce it to rest, which only can occur without loss of the reality which the emergent motion brings with it if we set in motion the other system with the emergent changes appearing in that system. In the case of General Relativity, Einstein undertook the task of formulating the universal conditions under which the changes in the spatio-temporal structure of the universe seem to take place —those changes which are due to motion, accelerated as well as unaccelerated. He has shown that these are also conditions for changes in mass, and is at work upon the task of showing that the same is true for electromagnetism.

Now the principle of sociality that I am attempting to enunciate is that in the present within which emergent change takes place the emergent object belongs to different systems in its passage from the old to the new because of its systematic relationship with other structures, and possesses the characters it has because of its membership in these different systems. While this principle has been evidenced most clearly in the doctrine of relativity as applied to physical theory, it is here least evident for our experience because the changes in mass, for example, due to the velocities with which we are familiar are so minute that the changes in Newton's law lie in the field of distant decimals. On the other hand electro-magnetic relativity has succeeded in presenting the form of the emergent with great exactness. We know the type of changes that will take place if any velocity appears within a certain system. Here we deal simply with the relation of the structures of space and time to motion. If we turn to the other two examples of sociality I have adduced—that of life and that of consciousness—we find ourselves in highly complex situations that are but dimly comprehended. We find that what understanding we have of life involves a reference to the future in the maintenance of the form and of the species. We know the life process is a physico-chemical process, but what the exact character of the process is we do not know as we know the character of a velocity. We do know, however, that the life processes are not confined to the organism, but taken as wholes include interactions between the organism and its surroundings, and we call that surrounding world, in so far as it is involved in these processes, the environment of the form and its species. That is, we recognize that emergent life changes the character of the world just as emergent velocities change the character of masses. And we know that what we call conscious processes are physiological processes, and that those processes which we generally call behavior utilize their organized adjustments in order to select the objects to which they respond, and that as a result of this behavior things within the environment of these living conscious forms take on values and meanings. We know that conscious processes are dependent upon a high development of an encephalon which is the outgrowth of the nervous mechanism of distance stimulation and of the delayed responses which distant stimuli make possible. The whole of such a nervous system provides both the field and the mechanism for selection with reference to distant futures, and this selection endows surrounding objects with the values and meanings which this future subtends. But what the physiological process is which puts at the disposal of the individual organism its highly organized responses for the purposes of discrimination and selection no one knows. There is, however, a great contrast between application of the principle of sociality in these different fields. In the field of physical relativity we know the process of motion with great exactness, but there are but three or four recondite experiments in which we can bring into our experience the effects which velocities have in changing the characters of things. On the other hand, the effects that result from living and conscious processes are evident on every side, while the nature of the processes has hitherto been shrouded in impenetrable obscurity. But in all three of these fields the principle of sociality nevertheless obtains. In all three there is emergence, and the character of this emergence is due to the presence in different systems of the same object or group of objects. Thus we find that in one system with certain space, time and energy characters, an object moving with a high velocity has an increased mass because it is characterized by different space, time and energy coefficients, and the whole physical system is thereby affected. In like manner, it is because an animal is both alive and a part of a physico-chemical world that life is an emergent and extends its influence to the environment about it. It is because the conscious individual is both an animal and is also able to look before and after that consciousness emerges with the meanings and values with which it informs the world.

CHAPTER IV

The Implications of the Self

I have indicated the position which I assume over against the so-called epistemological problem, namely, that knowing is an undertaking that always takes place within a situation that is not itself involved in the ignorance or uncertainty that knowledge seeks to dissipate. Knowledge is not then to be identified with the presence of content in experience. There is no conscious attitude that is as such cognitive. Knowledge is a process in conduct that so organizes the field of action that delayed and inhibited responses may take place. The test of the success of the process of knowledge, that is, the test of truth, is found in the discovery or construction of such objects as will mediate our conflicting and checked activities and allow conduct to proceed. Knowledge is inferential and always implies that a datum is involved in the inference. Reflection is the operation of inference in the field of ideation, i.e., the functioning as symbols of contents and characters of things, by means of which constructions of objects sought can be carried out.

Evidently ideation arises within what we term consciousness, and consciousness therefore calls for consideration. The lowest form of consciousness that we ascribe to living things is feeling. In general we do not judge that living forms without central nervous systems possess feeling, though there is difference of opinion on this. What naïve judgment comes back to is the evidence that response is called forth by what is good or bad for the animal. We assume acceptance and rejection, and ascribe pleasure and displeasure respectively to these two attitudes. There is evidence of acceptance and rejection even in the behavior of some unicellular forms, and we accordingly find biologists and psychologists ascribing consciousness in this lowest form even to these organisms. Pleasures and displeasures come under what we call organic experiences, at least in the situations to which I am referring, and our instinctive tendency to couple them with acceptance and rejection indicates an assumption that states of an animal's own organism enter into its experience. At this lowest limit of what we may call the emergence of consciousness we assume that the organism reacts to conditions in its own life process. So general a statement as this doubtless brings many of the reactions of plants within its sweep. What keeps plants out of our customary generalization, however, is the fact that plants do not react as a whole in their acceptances and rejections.

Thus the first condition of consciousness is life, a process in which the individual by its action tends to maintain this process both in itself and in later generations, and one which extends beyond what goes on in the organism out into the surrounding world and defines so much of the world as is found within the sweep of these activities as the environment of the individual. The second condition is that the living form in its teleological process can react, as a whole, purposively, to conditions of its own organism. However, I have defined emergence as the presence of things in two or more different systems, in such a fashion that its presence in a later system changes its character in the earlier system or systems to which it belongs. Hence, when we say that the lowest form of consciousness is feeling, what is implied is that when living forms enter such a systematic process that they react purposively and as wholes to their own conditions, consciousness as feeling arises within life. I have assumed that a certain systematic physico-chemical process arises which so selects what it reacts upon as to maintain the process, and that this process, appearing within the physical world, emerges as life. Into this situation there now comes a form that not only lives but makes its own organic conditions, favorable or unfavorable to life, part of the field to which it reacts or within which it lives. A conscious form is one that can make phases of its own life-process parts of its environment. An animal that selects certain of its own living states, as the rootlets of a plant select water when the plant needs water, not only lives, as does the plant, but is also thirsty. Feeling is the term we use for this added element in life, when the animal enters in some degree into its own environment.

Now the biological mechanism by which this seems to take place is the nervous system, for this not only enables the animal to select appropriate stimuli, but also makes the functioning of such surfaces of its own body as come into contact with the selected food a part of the object to which the animal responds. He not only ingests food, he also tastes it. I have also called emergence an expression of sociality. The animal is a part not only of the inanimate but also of the animate world: the conscious animal not only selects objects, but senses them as well. Thus, he is on the way to becoming part of the world within which he lives. The earlier form of consciousness lies in the field of contact experience. Here the animal responds to the object and in so doing responds to himself not as a whole, but only to the functioning of the contact surfaces. Later distance-stimuli come to be involved in his responses to his organic conditions and enter into the conscious field. The animal thus becomes more and more intimately a part of the world of objects about him. But the great advance comes with the development of the encephalon. This is primarily the nerve center of the important distance senses. As these become more powerful and refined in their discriminations, the contact experiences to which they respond are delayed, and possibilities of adjustment and of choice in response are thus increased. In the innervations of the attitudes that distant objects call out the animal feels the invitation or the threat they carry with them. He experiences his own repressed responses in his response to the distant stimulation. His responses to his own tendencies to act provide the control that organizes all his responses into a coördinated act, so that these inner feelings wax in importance in the development of the mechanism. Of equal importance is the separation, involved in the distance stimulation, between the content of the experience and the immediate response. It is here that we first meet the stuff of ideation. Of course in itself the distance stimulation is just that and nothing more. It is only as the organism gets itself into this distance stimulation that it comes into the field of so-called consciousness. It is from the awakening of delayed and mutually conflicting responses that the stuff for ideation is derived.

Let me state again the situation within which consciousness appears. Primarily living forms react to external stimulation in such fashion as to preserve the living process. The peculiar method that distinguishes their reactions from the motions of inanimate objects is that of selection. This selection is due to the sensitivity of the living form. Among inanimate processes the nearest approach to selection is catalysis. One may say that a living form is continually catalysing itself. Its own condition determines the objects and influences to which it will respond. The conscious animal carries selection into the field of its own response. It responds to the influence or effect the outer world has upon it. The immediate effect of food upon the animal is ingestion, and the peculiar character of life is exhausted in the animal's selection, through sensitization of the organism, of that substance to which it will respond—in other words, of its food. We can by mechanical devices sensitize a photographic plate. The structure of such a plate is maintained by mechanical forces. If a plate through the operation of these forces were to sensitize itself to light, it would be a living form. The operation of light upon an animal or plant is a photo-chemical process as mechanical as upon a kodak film. In the same manner the reaction of the form to the food-substance brought into contact with it is mechanical. As a living form it has selected what it will ingest, and mechanics takes care of the process of ingestion. But if in the process of ingestion the animal finds a stimulation to direct, to enhance or to inhibit this process, an activity of its own has become the object of its selection in maintaining the life process, that is in eating. In this case the animal has become conscious. The primary difficulty in dealing with these matters lies in our tendency to cut off life and consciousness at the boundaries of the organism. Selection undoubtedly lies in the living form, but such a form can only live in a physical environment of a definite sort. Living processes include active relationships with objects in an environment, and conscious living processes also include such objects. The response of the organism to its own response to food undoubtedly lies within the organism, but only as a part of a whole process of eating that includes also the food. To confine consciousness to the response of the organism to its food is not only to take it out of its setting but also to fail to recognize that it is only one phase of the eating. Conscious eating is tasting food, and to translate the tasting of food into other responses of the organism to its responses toward things not only involves a hopeless snarl but deprives such responses of all meaning. Life becomes conscious at those points at which the organism's own responses enter as part of the objective field to which it reacts.

This brings us to the sensory characters of things. The animal's conscious pleasure in the flavor of food is the state by which his organism responds to his eating of a food with certain characters. The selection of those characters of the food is part of the life process, and may be quite peculiar to a particular individual—*de gustibus non est disputandum.* Is the flavor his in the same sense in which the pleasure is his? The animal senses the flavor as really as he senses his own pleasure. The conscious phase of this sensory process lies in his use of selective discrimination in sniffing the food, but while the smelling is his, evidently the smell is not. But so far as his own responses get into the odorous object, that is, so far as this object is something to be seized or rejected, it is evidently an affair of consciousness. If we go farther than this and ask whether the color, or odor, or warmth, or smoothness of the object, apart from any response of the organism in the way of sensing it, belongs to the animal, we are probably asking two questions. The one question—whether the odor belongs to the organism as the pleasure does—we have already answered in the negative. The status of the pleasure would come nearest to what we mean by the phrase, "state of consciousness." The other—whether the so-called sensory quality apart from the sensing of it is a state of consciousness, as we have defined consciousness—is already answered; but the further implication that the sensory character would not be there if the animal were not there, takes us into the relation of the form to its environment. As parallel lines meeting at the horizon would not exist apart from some sort of optical apparatus leading to the convergence of the lines, so we may say that color would not exist apart from the apparatus of a retina and the mechanism behind it. The comparison is unfortunate because we can construct an optical apparatus with reference to which parallel lines do converge, while we cannot construct a retina with reference to which the world takes on colors. But what really lies back in our minds is the idea that the real surface is made up of vibrating molecules, so that the color cannot be on the object, and must be put into consciousness for lack of any other habitat. That vibrating molecules are not yellow surfaces is true. But that vibrating molecules may not exist as colored surfaces for animals with certain retinal apparatuses is not rendered impossible by that fact. There may be what we may call sensory perspectives as well as spatial and temporal perspectives. In any case, it means nothing to call color a state of consciousness, in the sense in which I have used consciousness.

And yet perceptual objects, with their sensuous qualities, belong to the realm of consciousness; for distance-experience exists as the promise or threat of contact-experience, and the way in which this future gets into the object is through the response of the organism to its own responses. In the perceptual world the future that is already there in the moving present is built out through the purposive responses of conscious organisms. The distant object thus comes to be what we can do to it or with it or by way of it or what it can do to us. To say that it exists instantaneously as we perceive it is but to demand confirmation of what is given in the perception. These purposive responses are there in the organism both as tendencies and as the results of past responses, and the organism responds to them in its perception. We frequently call this latter response imagery. Certainly much of what we perceive is made up of such imagery. In so far as it is distinguishable imagery, it is evidently of the same sort as the sensuous material of things, and so is marked as belonging to the present, and is spoken of as in the mind and as put into things. In dreams and hallucinations it is the largest part of our objects. Its relation to the nervous system is very obscure. Its appearance is presumably dependent upon conditions in the central nervous system due to past experiences, but it can no more be placed within the brain than can percepts; and if we may refer to the "stuff" of images, it is of the same sort as that of percepts. Imagery belongs to the perspective of the individual. He alone has access to it, and, finally, it is always stuff that has appeared in earlier perception. It constitutes a most important part of the environment of the human individual. It is however generally so merged with the objects and attitudes with which it functions, and, especially in speech, with incipient muscular reactions, that it is difficult to define and isolate it in our actual experience. It functions largely in the building out of the past and the future.

Ideas are closely related to images. They also have been regarded as sure evidence of a substantial mind postulated in order to provide them with a habitat. Since the symbols with which we think are largely recognized as word images, ideas and images have a very close consanguinity. The relationship is of course the same as that between a spoken or written word and its meaning; but, since the auditory or visual image of a word seems to be in the mind where the idea is placed, it is not uncommon, when we desire to distinguish between the words we use in speech and the meanings which they connote, to identify the meaning with the inner words with which we carry on our thinking. In any case one part of the idea as it appears in experience is some perceptual symbol, whether it is of the type of so-called imagery or of something seen or heard. The other part of the idea—the logician's and metaphysician's universal—comes back to what I have referred to as attitudes or organized responses selecting characters of things when they can be detached from the situations within which they take place. Particularly do our habitual responses to familiar objects constitute for us the ideas of these objects. The definitions we give of them are the sure signs by which we can arouse identical or like attitudes in others. I am not interested in the logical or metaphysical problems they have called out, but in the fact that as organized responses of the organism they do enter into the experience we call conscious. That is, the organism responds to these organized attitudes in their relations to objects as it does to other parts of its world. And thus these become objects for the individual.

Now it is by these ideational processes that we get hold of the conditions of future conduct as these are found in the organized responses which we have formed, and so construct our pasts in anticipation of that future. The individual who can thus get hold of them can further organize them through the selection of the stimulations which call them out and can thus build up his plan of action. It is my contention that the past is always constructed in this fashion and therefore always with reference to the situation which calls out this deliberative attitude. I have been merely detailing the conditions in an emergent evolution which have made such deliberative situations possible.

In dealing with sociality I have laid stress upon the passage in emergence from the old system to the new, emphasizing the fact that in this passage the emergent lies in both, and is what it is because it carries the characters of both at once. Thus a moving body has an increase in mass over against the system within which it is moving, a living organism has a selective power in maintenance of the life process in the midst of inanimate things, and a conscious individual reacts to his own responses. He thus gains a new type of control in the maintenance of the living organism, and invests with values the objects of his environment. The other dimension of sociality, where this term expresses the determination of the nature of an object by the natures of other objects belonging to the same system, is evident in the conception of energy systems, in the development of multicellular forms in which the life of the whole system is the integrated life of the differentiated cells that make it up, in the social systems involved in the propagation of the species and in the integration of societies, from those in which at first balance is reached between reproduction and the consumption of one form by another, up to those in which a social process is mediated by differentiation of individuals. In all these the nature of the individual is in varying degrees the expression of the natures of other members of the system or society.

The difference between these two dimensions of sociality is temporal. A system can conceivably be taken at an instant, and the social character of the individual member would in that instant be what it is because of the mutual relationships of all members. On the other hand, an object can be a member of two divergent systems only in passage, in which its nature in one system leads to the transformation which its passing into another system carries with it. In the passage itself it can be in both. I have sufficiently illustrated this in the case of change of mass with increase in velocity. In the case of living forms we are as a rule presented with a *fait accompli.* The situation in which there exists a cell living its own life and finding itself commencing to live the life of a multicellular form must have arisen in the evolution of these forms, but the origin of such a situation we can only dimly trace in embryonic development where the higher rate of nutrition of certain cells in comparison with that of others appears to lead to differentiation. As a further example we may consider the instant at which the material we now know as the sun first took on its planetary nature, or that at which, under tidal and other influences, a double star appears.

The striking fact in relativity is that changes in spatio-temporal and energy dimensions are not starting-points of new structures. There must be some change in those systems in which a body increases in mass, but these are not incident to new orders. The differences, so to speak, are cancelled by corresponding changes in other systems. It is this situation that so strongly favors the assumption of a reality lying behind the different perspectives, to which the reality of experiences under different frames of reference belongs—a Minkowski space-time with its events and intervals. There is, however, another possibility in the case of relativity with its different perspectives, viz., that of occupying in experience alternative systems. Whitehead for example refers to a double consciousness of cogredience, in which the observer identifies himself both with the space-time of a train and with that of the landscape through which the train is moving. Evidently relativity as a doctrine would have been impossible but for this type of consciousness. Einstein's doctrine has been called one of signals. It involves the realization of different meanings of the spatio-temporal order of events in different systems at the same time. Now I have presented consciousness as the response of an organism to its own responses, with the corresponding change which the environment undergoes in its meanings. The world is a different world to one man from what it is to another, as is illustrated by the fact that a dollar means one thing to one man and a different thing to another. The man who can take both points of view is able to order and price his goods successfully. Out of this capacity there arises an abstract value for the dollar as a means of exchange—a value which it has in the worlds of all three. The Minkowski world should be such a meaning attaching to actual experiences of persons in different systems moving with reference to each other, but it does not so appear. It appears rather as a system of transformations and the constants that shake out of them, where these are made into symbols of entities that cannot enter into experience. In older views of relativity, differences in perspectives due to motion could be translated from one system to another with the same relative change in the position of the objects. There was no change in the character of the object in one because of its motion in the other. Usually there was a preferred system to which all others were transformed for common comprehension. So we could take the coördinates of the fixed stars as a basis for understanding the motions of the stars with reference to our system. What was common to all systems was the identical relative positions of the objects. Electro-magnetic relativity, on the other hand, has shown a difference in the spatio-temporal and energy dimensions of things in motion with reference to the system within which they move, so that we cannot simply translate from one to the other, and especially we cannot set up any common structure of the things in whatever system they may be. The mathematical apparatus for transformation becomes very complicated.

The metaphysical question is, can a thing with changing spatio-temporal and energy dimensions be the same thing with different dimensions, when we have seemingly only these dimensions by which to define the thing? It has seemed simpler to say that the real thing lies behind these experiences which are subjective and phenomenal. But let us instead accept passage as the character of reality, and recognize that in passage there is change in the structure of things, and that because of passage objects can occupy different systems. If we then recognize that there is a form of sociality within which we can go from the one to the other by means of a system of transformations, and so occupy both systems, identifying the same objects in each, it becomes possible for passage to take place between alternative systems that are simultaneously mutually exclusive. The set of transformations and the mathematical structure built upon it are as much parts of nature as anything else. They are attitudes answering to meanings of things brought under our control by symbols. Passage from a system in motion to the same system at rest, while the rest of world passes from rest to motion, means passage from the one to the other in what we call a mind. These two aspects exist in nature, and the mind is also in nature. The mind passes from one to the other in its so-called consciousness, and the world is a different world from the standpoint of one attitude from what it is from another. We say the world cannot occupy both meanings, if they are mutually exclusive; but passage in a mind enables it to do so by means of transformations. All that we need to recognize is that the world had the one aspect from one point of view and that it now has the other aspect from another point of view, and that there has been the same passage in nature from the one to the other as has taken place in the mind, just as there is a passage from one price to another in stocks on the market because of the changing attitudes in men's minds.

The question at issue here is, what is there in nature that answers to the transformation in the mathematician's mind? If we accept mind as existing in nature and recognize that mind, by means of the temporal dimension in sociality, passes from one system to another, so that the objects to which the mathematician refers in one system appear in the other in different spatio-temporal and energy dimensions, by means of transformation formulae; and recognize also that the minded organism has the other dimension of sociality as well, so that what appears now as in one system and now within another, lies, since it has an identical character to the organism, in a system in the world answering to this character of the minded organism; then we can assume that the reference of the constants in these different perspectives is not to entities outside possible experience but to this organized character of the world that appears in what we call mind. To state the matter less cumbrously, the relativist is able to hold on to two or more mutually exclusive systems within which the same object appears, by passing from one to the other. I have already referred to the experiential form of this passage in which the man in a train passes from the system of the movement of his train to that of the movement of a neighboring train. His train cannot be both moving and at rest, but the mind of the passenger can occupy in passage both systems, and hold the two attitudes in a comprehensible relationship to each other as representing the same occurrence from two different standpoints which, having a mind or being a mind, he can occupy. If he accepts the two mutually exclusive situations as both legitimate, it is because as a minded organism he can be in both.

It is to such an organization of perspectives that the constants in the mathematics of relativity may refer. We state this summarily, and with avoidance of philosophical complications, by saying that these mathematics give us a more accurate method of formulating and measuring the physical world; but this still leaves the seeming contradiction of an object possessing at the same time differing spatio-temporal and energy dimensions, when it is only by these that the object can be defined. There would be no difficulty if we could set up one definition as the correct one and refer others to illusory factors—we should then simply regard our own train as moving. We do the same sort of a thing when we say that the two systems are simply the structure which the objects have under different frames of reference. Both are then illusory. But in this case we must relegate the reality to a Minkowski world. My contention is that they are both real for a mind that can occupy in passage both systems. The other illustration which I have given is that of price in the economic world; but I have indicated the difference that both individuals in the different perspectives here come back to a common entity of price in terms of exchange, which, in the form of money, is an identical affair for each, while the two individuals in the systems moving with reference to each other cannot find such common realities in their experience. They get instead a set of transformation-formulae. What they come back to is what Russell refers to as a common logical pattern, and what I am maintaining is that two individuals in the systems which Einstein presents, connected with each other by light signals so that each individual places himself in the system of the other as well as in his own, are living in a common world, and that a reference to a Minkowski world is unnecessary. Individuals living together in such systems would soon carry with them constantly these two definitions of everything, just as we carry two systems of time when travelling. What would be impossible would be the reduction of this common world to an instant. The temporal dimension of sociality is essential to its existence. One cannot be in Chicago and Berkeley at the same instant even in thought; but even if we did not have the same earth under us, which can be the same at an instant, we could hold in our passing present in thought a common life. I have clung to this illustration because it presents an extreme example of the organization of perspectives which sociality accomplishes in both of its dimensions when they can appear in minded organisms.

The self by its reflexive form announces itself as a conscious organism which is what it is only so far as it can pass from its own system into those of others, and can thus, in passing, occupy both its own system and that into which it is passing. That this should take place is evidently not the affair of a single organism. Shut up within his own world—that which answers to his stimulations and responses—he would have no entrance into possibilities other than those which his own organized act involved. It is only as his activity is a part of a larger organized process that such a possibility can open. Nor is this the only prerequisite. The social organization of a multicellular form is one in which each cell in living its own life lives the life of the whole; but its differentiation restricts its expressions to the single function to which it has become adapted. Only in a process in which one organism can in some sense substitute for another could an individual find itself taking the attitude of another while still occupying its own. Its own differentiation must never be so complete as to restrict it to fulfilling a single function only. It is the high degree of physiological differentiation among insects that presumably precludes their highly organized communities from reaching self-consciousness.

There remains the mechanism by which the individual living his own life in that of the group is placed in the attitude of taking the rôle of another. That mechanism is, of course, that of communication. There may be a type of communication in which the condition of one organ stimulates others to their appropriate responses. There is in the physiological system such a system of communication carried out by the hormones. But this is only an elaboration of the interrelation of highly differentiated organs functioning in a common life-process. Communication as I shall use it always implies the conveyance of meaning; and this involves the arousal in one individual of the attitude of the other, and his response to these responses. The result is that the individual may be stimulated to play various parts in the common process in which all are engaged, and can therefore face the various futures which these different rôles carry with them, in reaching finally the form that his own will take. Thus the life of the community to which he belongs becomes a part of his experience in a higher sense than would be possible for a differentiated organ within an organic whole. The final step in the development of communication is reached when the individual that has been aroused to take the rôles of others addresses himself in their rôles, and so acquires the mechanism of thinking, that of inward conversation. The genesis of mind in human society I will not here discuss. What I wish to bring out in the first place is that it is a natural development within the world of living organisms and their environment. Its first characteristic is consciousness, that emergent which arises when the animal passes from the system in which it formerly existed to an environment that arises through the selectiveness of its own sensitivity, and thus to a new system within which parts of its own organism and its reactions to these parts become parts of its environment. The next step is reached with the dominance of the distance senses and the delayed responses to these. The selection and organization of these responses, together with the characters of the objects which they have selected, now become objects within the environment of the organism. The animal comes to respond to an environment consisting largely of possible futures of its own delayed reactions, and this inevitably emphasizes its own past responses in the form of acquired habits. These pass into the environment as the conditions of his acts. These characters of the environment constitute the stuff out of which values and meanings later arise, when these characters can be isolated through gestures in communication. The systems to which I have referred are in all cases interrelations between the organism and the world that reveals itself as environment, determined by its relationship to the organism.

Any essential change in the organism brings with it a corresponding change in the environment.

The passage, then, from one system into another is the occasion for an emergence both in the form and in the environment. The development in animal life has been steadily toward bringing more and more of the activity of the animal within the environment to which it responds, by the growth of a nervous system through which it could respond both to its sense processes and also to its responses to these, in its whole life activity. But the animal could never reach the goal of becoming an object to itself as a whole until it could enter into a larger system within which it could play various rôles, so that in taking one rôle it could stimulate itself to play the other rôle which this first rôle called for. It is this development that a society whose life process is mediated by communication has made possible. It is here that mental life arises—with this continual passing from one system to another, with the occupation of both in passage and with the systematic structures that each involves. It is the realm of continual emergence.

I have wished to present mind as an evolution in nature, in which culminates that sociality which is the principle and the form of emergence. The emergence in nature of sensuous qualities is due to the fact that an organ can respond to nature in differing systematic attitudes and yet occupy both attitudes. The organism responds to itself as affected by the tree and at the same time to the tree as the field of its possible future reactions. The possibility of the organism being at once in three different systems, that of physical relation, of vital relation and of sensuous relation, is responsible for the appearance of the colored rough shaft and foliage of the tree emerging in the interrelation between the object and the organism. But mind in its highest sense involves the passage from one attitude to another with the consequent occupation of both. This also takes place in nature. It is the phase of change in which both states are found in the process. An acceleration in velocity is the outstanding illustration of this situation, and the whole development of our modern physical science has been dependent upon our isolation of this entity in change. But while this concurrent occupation of different situations at once occurs in nature, it has remained for mind to present a field within which the organism not only passes from one attitude to another and so occupies both, but also holds on to this common phase. One can pass from the situation within which a dog appears, to that in which a toad appears, and so on to an elephant, and be in all attitudes at once in so far as they all include the common attitude toward "an animal." Now this is the highest expression of sociality, because the organism not only so passes from one attitude to another, by means of a phase which is a part of all these attitudes, but also comes back on itself in the process and responds to this phase. It must get out of itself in the passage and react to this factor in the passage.

I have indicated the mechanism by which this is accomplished. It is that of a society of organisms which become selves, first of all taking the attitudes of others to themselves, and then using the gestures by which they have conversed with others to indicate to themselves what is of interest in their own attitudes. I will not spend time in discussing this fascinating field of mental development.[1] I wish to emphasize the fact that the appearance of mind is only the culmination of that sociality which is found throughout the universe, its culmination lying in the fact that the organism, by occupying the attitudes of others, can occupy its own attitude in the rôle of the other. A society is a

---

[1] Cf. pages 200 ff.

systematic order of individuals in which each has a more or less differentiated activity. The structure is really there in nature, whether we find it in the society of bees or that of human beings. And it is in varying degrees reflected in each individual. But, as I have already stated, it can get into the separate individual only in so far as he can take the parts of others while he is taking his own part. It is due to the structural organization of society that the individual, in successively taking the rôles of others in some organized activity, finds himself selecting what is common in their interrelated acts, and so assumes what I have called the rôle of the generalized other. This is the organization of those common attitudes which all assume in their varied responses. It may be that of a mere human being, that of the citizen of a definite community, that of the members of a club, or that of a logician in his "universe of discourse." A human organism does not become a rational being until he has achieved such an organized other in his field of social response. He then carries on that conversation with himself which we call thought, and thought, as distinct from perception and imagination, is occupied with indicating what is common in the passage from one attitude to another. Thus thought reaches what we call universals, and these, with the symbols by which they are indicated, constitute ideas.

Now this is possible only in the continual passage from attitude to attitude; but the fact that we do not remain simply in this passage is due to our coming back upon it in the rôle of the self and organizing the characters which we pick out into the patterns this social structure of the self puts at our disposal. The stretch of the present within which this self-consciousness finds itself is delimited by the particular social act in which we are engaged. But since this usually stretches beyond the immediate perceptual horizon we fill it out with memories and imagination. In the whole undertaking these serve in place of perceptual stimulations to call out the appropriate responses. If one is going to meet an appointment, he indicates to himself the streets he must traverse by means of their memory images or the auditory images of their names. And this involves both the past and the future. In a sense his present takes in the whole undertaking, but it can accomplish this only by using symbolic imagery, and since the undertaking is a whole that stretches beyond the immediate specious presents, these slip into each other without any edges. A loud noise behind one's back picks out such a specious present. Its lack of relevance to what is going on leaves it nothing but the moment in which the sound vibrated within our ears. But our functional presents are always wider than the specious present, and may take in long stretches of an undertaking which absorbs unbroken concentrated attention. They have ideational margins of varying depth, and within these we are continually occupied in the testing and organizing process of thought. The functional boundaries of the present are those of its undertaking—of what we are doing. The pasts and futures indicated by such activity belong to the present. They arise out of it and are criticized and tested by it. The undertakings belong, however, with varying degrees of intimacy, within larger activities, so that we seldom have the sense of a set of isolated presents.

I wish to make as emphatic as possible the reference of pasts and futures to the activity that is central to the present. Ideation extends spatially and temporally the field within which activity takes place. The presents, then, within which we live are provided with margins, and fitting them into a larger independent chronicle is again a matter of some more extended present which calls for a wider horizon. But the widest horizon belongs to some undertaking, whose past and future refer back to it. For instance, the present history of the sun is relevant to the undertaking of unravelling the atom and, given another analysis of the atom, the sun will have another history and the universe will be launched into a new future. The pasts and the futures are implications of what is being undertaken and carried out in our laboratories.

It is interesting to note the lack of historic significance in Aristotle's account of the universe. At most there were the pulses of reproduction or of the succession of the seasons. Its past had no other function than that of repetition. Even Plato's Day of Judgment was a recurrent affair. In the highest reality—thought thinking itself—past and future fade out entirely, as they do in the contemplation of timeless reality in a Platonic heaven. St. Paul and Augustine ushered in the history of the world, which gave a defined cosmical horizon to the undertaking of every soul in its search for salvation from the wrath to come, or for the beatific vision. The Bible and the monuments of the church became the chronicle of Christendom, for in them men found the means of salvation. It was not until scientific research became an independent undertaking that it was possible to substitute another chronicle. But the import of the biblical history was found not only in the salvation of men's souls. The Church was the structure of Western society and the undertaking to conserve the values of this society found its essential past and future in the plan of salvation. It is this larger undertaking to which as social beings we are committed that provides to-day the horizons of our pasts and future. But this undertaking includes among its values the work of research science and the implications of that rational process which has freed us from the isolation of individual organisms and made us not only members of the Blessed Community but also citizens of the republic of all rational beings. But even in the sweep of these most universal undertakings, their pasts and their futures are still relative to the interests involved in the undertakings themselves. We determine what the world has been by the anxious search for the means of making it better, and we are substituting the goal of a society aware of its own values and minded intelligently to pursue them, for the city not built with hands eternal in the heavens.

This view then frees us from bondage either to past or future. We are neither creatures of the necessity of an irrevocable past, nor of any vision given in the Mount. Our history and our prognostications will be sympathetic with the undertakings within which we live and move and have our being. Our values lie in the present, and past and future give us only the schedule of the means, and the plans of campaign, for their realization.

We live always in a present whose past and whose future are the extension of the field within which its undertakings may be carried out. This present is the scene of that emergence which gives always new heavens and a new earth, and its sociality is the very structure of our minds. Since society has endowed us with self-consciousness, we can enter personally into the largest undertakings which the intercourse of rational selves extends before us. And because we can live with ourselves as well as with others, we can criticize ourselves, and make our own the values in which we are involved through those undertakings in which the community of all rational beings is engaged.

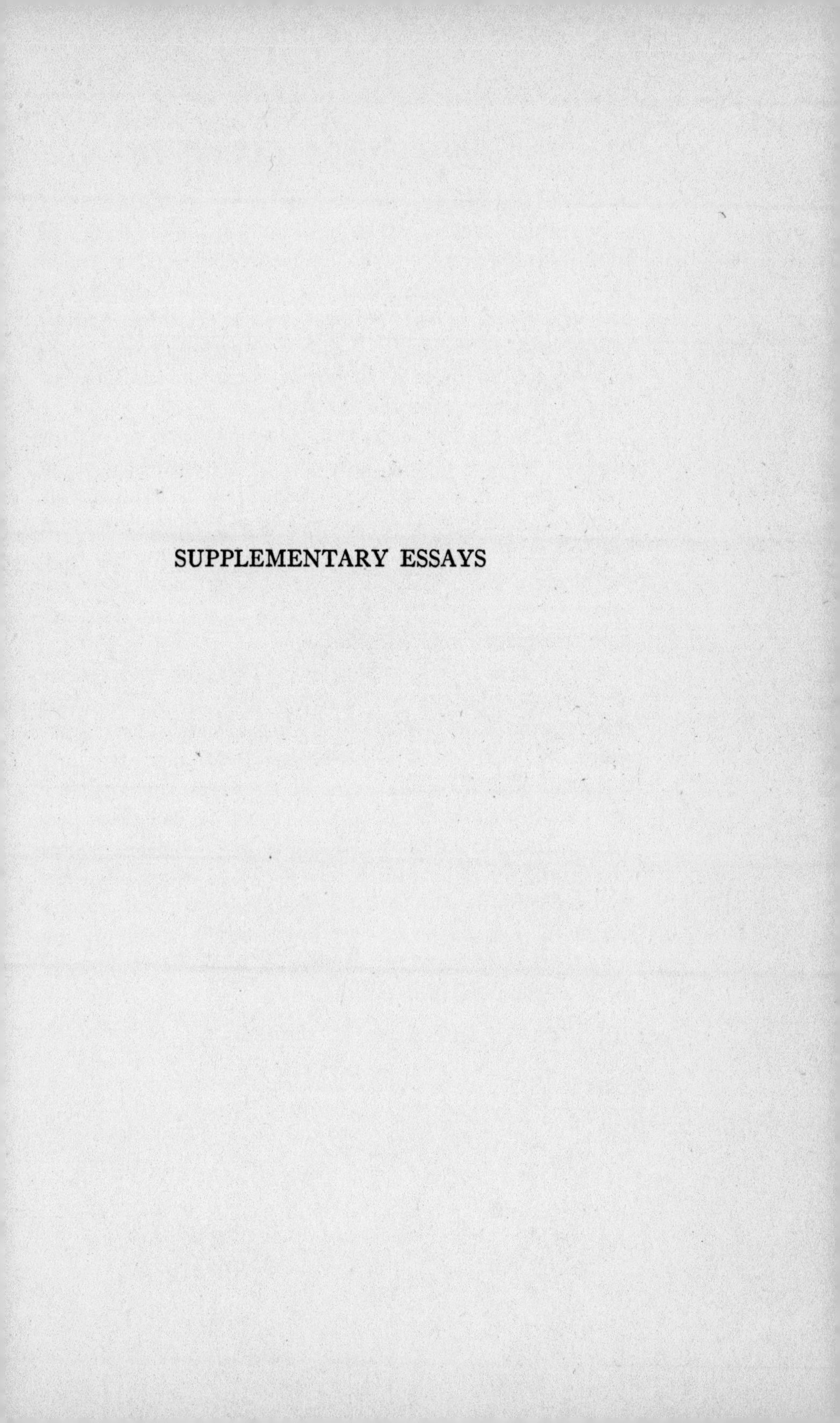

SUPPLEMENTARY ESSAYS

SUPPLEMENTARY ESSAYS

I

Empirical Realism

There are two points of incidence of any act of knowledge: the deduction of what must occur in experience if the idea we entertain is true, and the reconstruction of the world which the acceptance of the idea involves. Thus, in the theory of relativity, the calculation of the apparent positions of stars close to the rim of the eclipsed sun and the agreement of the calculations of the theory with the revolution of the orbit of Mercury are illustrations of the first. Einstein's theory of a curved space-time or Whitehead's doctrine of intersecting time-systems is an illustration of the second. Barring errors of observation, the so-called experimental proofs remain as data under any alternative theory, while the reconstructed world that arises out of the theory is never in its own right definitive. A new theory will reconstruct this as it has reconstructed its predecessor.

It is interesting to note that this difference in the definitive value of data and of theories under which data are organized and from which they gain new meanings is not due to a higher degree of competence in reaching them. The more competently data are isolated and observed the more likely they are to remain as secure elements in the formulation and solution of later problems; but the logical perfection of a theory and its wide applicability have no bearing upon the likelihood of its survival in the presence of new problems. This is clearly evidenced in the attitude of present-day physicists toward Newtonian mechanics. In fact the very perfection and comprehensiveness of an hypothesis lessen its survival value in the face of fundamental problems. Scientists find themselves in possession of a constantly increasing body of reliable data, while the very character of their research-undertakings calls for a constant reinterpretation of the world within which their research goes on.

What bearing has this upon the scientist's realism, upon his assurance that there is an intelligible world *there* over against his investigation? Such a phenomenalist as Mach finds his reality in the data, and is or should be ready to recognize new uniformities among them without feeling that his field of reality has changed. He can regard things and the world made of things as mere convenient and subjective orderings of data which can be rearranged without affecting the only reality with which science is concerned. But our constructive scientists are not phenomenalists. Einstein condemns phenomenalism[1] and among theorists such as Eddington, Weyl, Minkowski, or Whitehead we find no phenomenalist. Technicians such as Rutherford, Bohr, Sommerfeld, Planck, or Schroeder, can state their findings only in terms of things and a world of things, however far removed from perceptual experience.

Data are isolated elements in a world of things. Their isolation is overcome in the new world of the scientist's hypothesis, and it is in this world that the reality lies which he is seeking. He cannot stop with the data in his cognitive advance. They belong to a stage in the investigation which comes before the attainment of knowledge. However uncertain he may be of the achievement, his impulse is not satisfied until the data have taken on the form of things in some sort of an ordered whole. These things may be removed from our perceptual experience and lie in a mathematical or logical intuition belonging to the expert only;

---

[1] Cf. Meyerson, "La Déduction Relativiste," pages 61-62.

but it is a world made up of objects, not of data, to which his hypothesis gives at least a provisional reality not attaching to them as mere data.

A further trait of the scientist's reality is its independence of the observer. This is strikingly illustrated, in the doctrine of relativity, by the geometry of space-time. An absolute independent of the frames of reference of all observers was an inevitable goal of the most fundamental criticism of commonsense spatial and temporal experience. However ready the scientist has been to recognize the perspectivity of all perception, he has never been infected by those scepticisms that have arisen from such recognition in philosophic doctrine. He has recognized far more adequately than the layman the insurmountable obstacles that defend the cognizable world from any complete comprehension by his science; but he has never relegated the object of his knowledge to the creations of his own perceptions and thought. He has always assumed the existence of something independent of his perception, and of the thought with which his research is occupied. It is this independence which underwrites his experiment. But this reality independent of the perception and thought of the observer is not presented in the data of science, apart from the world to which such data belong. These data are perceptual experiences, isolated by the problem within which they appear, and occurring under such exacting conditions that they can be counted upon to be repeated not only in the scientist's own experience but also, under similar conditions, in that of others. In no case would the independent reality be identified with the refined measurement of points on a photographic plate, or with the observations of an astronomer, in so far as these are in contradiction to current doctrine. It is these latter which constitute the data of science. Independent reality belongs either to the world in so far as not affected by the problem, or to a reconstituted world. The observations are indications of the necessity of reconstitution, and evidences of the legitimacy of an hypothesis by which such reconstitution is undertaken; but in the form of data they cannot belong to a reconstituted world. Such a world is a system of intelligible things whose meanings have wiped out the isolation of the data, and perhaps have removed their import from the perceptual experience within which they occurred.

We are thus brought back to the intelligible reality that is the fundamental assumption of the scientist's undertaking. I have already referred to the meaning of the intelligibility of reality in the scientist's quest for knowledge. It is found in the possibility of deducing, from determining conditions of events as given in experience, what the nature of those events must be. There are, then, two assumptions involved in such intelligibility: (1) that events in their passage are determined, although the degree of this determination is not fixed by the assumption; and (2) that in so far as the determining conditions are given, the character of later events is also given. There is, however, a difference between the givenness of the determining conditions and the givenness of the later events. The former is that of the temporal dimension of experience. But while there is in all passage determination—in abstract phraseology the carrying on of relations—there is also the indeterminateness of what occurs. There is always qualitative difference in passage, as well as identity of relation extending through passage. The "what" that is occurring is given in this relational aspect only. In this lies the rationality of all experience, and the source of symbolism. It is here also that we find the fundamental distinction between the objective and subjective phases of experience. The carrying on of relations is objective. The anticipated qualitative "what" that will occur is subjective. Its locus is mind. Here we find the second sort of givenness—that which belongs to later events. In so far as the relations in the passage are there in experience they pass in their identity into further events, but the "what" that will occur is only symbolically present. And the indeterminate "what" involves always a possibly new situation with a new complex of relationships. The givenness of later events is then the extension of the structure of relations found in experience, in which the event can be defined only in its relational import, though we imaginatively anticipate with varying degrees of probability its qualitative character. The intelligibility of the world is found in this structure of relations which are there in experience, and in the possibility of following them on beyond the specious present into a future in so far as this future is determined. The data are such emergent events as fail to fit into the accepted structure of relations, and become nodal points from which a new structure of relations arises. They thus are isolated, though they lie within a world which has not been entirely disrupted. It is in their isolation that they are interesting; and while they are defined in terms of objective relations which are not affected, it is in their opposition to previously accepted meanings that they must be presented. A relatum that hangs in the air without as yet the structure of relations to which it belongs is given in a type of experience which can embody both its inherence in a world that is there and its contradiction of certain characters of that world.[2] The Michelson-Morley findings are an illustration of this type of experience. The interference rings were unchanged, whether the light waves travelled with the motion of the earth or at right angles to it. Motions were simply

[2]For a much more extended discussion see Mr. Mead's essay on "Scientific Method and the Individual Thinker" in "Creative Intelligence," page 176 ff.

there in a world of exact measurement which was the condition of any experiment. But they were in flagrant opposition to the assumption that these waves travelled in an ether unaffected by that motion, occupying the Newtonian space of current physical doctrine. The unquestioned thereness of these rings in their unexpected conflict with the character of the spatial world to which they had belonged expresses the data's independence of certain characters of that experience in so far as they are in conflict with these findings.

There is an old quarrel between rationalism and empiricism which can never be healed as long as either sets out to tell the whole story of reality. Nor is it possible to divide the narrative between them. When rationalism tells the tale, the goal is a Parmenidean identity; when empiricism tells it, reality disappears in phenomenalistic sands. But in fact contingency presupposes a universal necessary order that has been transgressed, and we achieve universal law only when we have triumphed over exceptions. Empiricism presents the ever-recurrent problem with its hard recalcitrant fact; rationalism, the verified theory in which it disappears. For example, the interpretation of things as events causes "things" to disappear in the geometry of a space-time which is the modern edition of the rationalism of Descartes. Neither the Minkowski space-time, nor Whitehead's intersections of an infinite number of time-systems with the ingression of eternal objects, opens the door to any reality in the perceptual findings of research science. For research science, perceptual findings are part of a world whose unquestioned security is the basis for the reality of the exceptional instance from which the problem springs, and for the reliability of the experimental verification of the later hypothesis; yet they have lost the meaning which had belonged to that world but which the exceptional instance has now annulled. The world was implicitly rational up to the advent of the problem. It is again rational once the problem is solved. The hard facts of the exceptional instance in observation and experiment have a reality independent of that rationality. To say that their reality is found in the faith that the world nevertheless is rational, is to substitute an emotional state for the immediate datum which asserts itself against a rational order and conceivably might maintain itself even in an irrational universe. It is essential to the scientist's method and attitude that he accept his findings just in their contravening of what had been their meaning, and as real in independence of whatever theory is advanced to explain them. Otherwise they would have no probative power. Such instances, with the problems they involve, constitute the contingency of the scientist's world. They are in the nature of the case unpredictable, and they are in the nature of the case real in spite of their non-rationality. It is also true that every consistent hypothesis rules out all later exceptions to its uniformity, or rather that it will be demolished by any exceptional instance. It is therefore no argument against the geometry of space-time that it opens no door to the contingent. No formally rational doctrine can include within itself the repugnant fact. But it is another matter to give such an account of reality as has within it no place for the authority of new scientific findings. The scientist who welcomes facts that fail to accord with his theory must have a place in his doctrine for the experience within which those facts can appear. Nor can we account for the repugnant fact, for the emergent, by relegating it to an experience that is simply that of a mind that has made a mistake or been in error and now corrects it with a true or at least a truer account of reality. The repugnant fact is without doubt an emergent; it has, however, been customary to place its essential novelty in a mental experience, and to deny it to the world that the mind is experiencing.

Thus radiation from black bodies presented facts repugnant to the formulation of light in terms of a wave process. Presumably an hypothesis will be found in which this repugnancy will disappear. Meantime, we do not question the facts, once they have been tested by approved technique. This comes back to pointer-readings; but we are apt to overlook the fact that pointer-readings involve very complex and extensive apparatus together with the physical housing of this apparatus—the whole perceptual world that is not involved in the doctrine of radiation—and that the facts are but parts of that perceptual world. In that world the pointer readings are emergents. From the scientist's standpoint this world is not mental. Is the emergence of the quanta mental? The Einsteinian must answer yes to this question. There can be no novelty in the geometry of an extension in which time is simply one dimension. In our different frames of reference we happen upon events and all the freshness of novelty is in the adventurer. Whitehead does locate the perspective of the organism within the world with which the scientist deals, and undertakes to open the door to contingency by way of alternative patterns of eternal objects which may have ingression into the perspective, or particular intersections of time systems dependent upon the percipient event. But this logical separation of the event—the occurrence—from the characters of the event—the "what it is" that takes place—finds no reflection in the scientist's object. The "what the object is" reflects its characters in its occurrence. If there is contingency in the selection of eternal objects, that contingency surely appears in the happening. Not only etymologically but logically contingency attaches itself to occurrence. Yet from the standpoint of Whitehead's doctrine the event is as unalterably located in a space-time as in the Einsteinian doctrine.

The scientist's emergent appears in his observation of the

repugnant fact. Unquestionably in his experience something novel has occurred, and his experience lies within the world. He is then interested in establishing as a fact that what is novel in his experience is also firmly imbedded in an unquestioned perceptual world. In so far as it is novel—e.g., in so far as the radiation of the black body does not conform to the wave theory of radiation—the new fact exists only as his experimental finding, as his perceptual experience, and he must make sure that any other person under like circumstances will have the same perceptual experience. The reality of this experience of his, and of others carrying out the like experiment, in its opposition to current meanings, is the cornerstone of experimental science. The novel fact is no mere sensation of the scientist, nor any mental state, but something that is happening to things that are real. In its repugnancy to a certain structural character of that world it arises only in the experience of this, that and the other individual; but these experiences must nevertheless belong to an unquestioned objective world. It is important to recognize that this world is not made up out of these individual experiences. They lie within this world. If it were made up of such individual experiences it would lose all its reality; whereas in fact it is a court of final appeal—there is no scientific theory that does not seek its decision, and there is no theory that may not be brought before it. It is entirely conceivable that facts repugnant to the current doctrine of relativity may appear, and it is the anticipation of research science that such will be the case.

It is customary to interpret the independence of data as a metaphysical affirmation of a real world independent of all observation and speculation. There is no necessary implication of this in the scientist's methodology. For the metaphysical affirmation is of a reality that is final, while the scientist's procedure and method contemplate no such finality. On the contrary, they contemplate continued reconstruction in the face of events emerging in ceaseless novelty. The scientist's method and technique are those of research. Unless his metaphysical predisposition leads him to identify the unquestioned thereness of the data with the finality of a world metaphysically independent of all experience, he cannot discover this finality in the data; for their very form moves toward a doctrine that will relieve them of the character of data and merge them in things. It is only in the identity of the relation in passage that he can find a character which could belong to such a final world. But, as Meyerson has pointed out,[3] such a reflection of reality in the identities that scientific method seeks leads only to a Parmenidean solid.

It is of course possible to approach the problem from the standpoint of this relational structure. Modern mathematics and relational logic are outstanding illustrations of this approach. The first step was taken in the Renaissance, in the freeing of the numerical relations of geometrical elements from the forms of perceptual intuition. Descartes' Analytic Geometry not only opened the door to the powerful instrument of analysis, but also freed the qualitative content of the object of observation from the common-sense structure of things. Scientific analysis was then free to attack the problems of physics and chemistry with the instruments of molecules and atoms, which could be defined in terms of the equations of mechanics. Justification for the hypothetical constructions this made possible could be found in the logical deductions of the theory when these were put to the test of experiment. It was mathematical analysis that freed the modern mind from Aristotelian metaphysics, by giving men new objects that could be exactly defined in

[3]"Identity and Reality," page 231.

terms of relational structures and then bringing these structures to the test of observation, through the deduction of their consequences. The profound distinction between the atomic elements of ancient and those of modern thought lies in the exact definition which modern science gives to its ultimate elements in terms of the mathematical account of the proportions they must submit to and of the changes they must undergo. An Aristotelian science could give no definition of the elements of things except the nature of the things as they lay in experience. There was no method open to the thinker except that of the metaphysics of potentiality and realization. Elements could be thought of only in terms of what they were to become. In the atom of Democritus, weight was an ultimate quality which was conceived as a cause of motion and of changes in motion; but the cause had nothing in common with the effect. It was not possible to utilize the analysis of motion into velocities, accelerations and decelerations and then define the weight—the dominant character of the atom—in terms of these determinable elements of motion. Weight was one character and the changes it brought about were other characters. The one could not be defined in terms of the other.

But when mass could be defined in terms of inertia and this in terms of the tendency of a body to remain in a state of rest or motion and in terms of the character of the motion in which it is found, it became possible to use the mathematical account of motion to define both the body and any part of it that this analysis rendered accessible to thought and experiment. It is not simply that there arose a new set of concepts for defining things, but that the situations arising from the mathematical analysis involved relational formulations of the objects. Both the inadequacy of the Cartesian mechanical doctrine and the striking success of Newtonian mechanics emphasized the importance of the new physical objects that had arisen out of a mathematical dynamics. Their indifference to the teleological natures of things in human experience rendered them peculiarly serviceable for fashioning means for new human ends. Newtonian mechanics gave man a control over nature from a source of which Bacon had not dreamed.

Of equal if not of greater importance was the experimental proof which the exact deduction of consequences from the mathematically formulated hypothesis offered to the scientist. Here was a *mathesis* which instead of withdrawing into a Platonic world of forms came back to a perceptual world that could be submitted to exact measurement, and found here final support. And again and again the development of mathematical theory has provided the structure within which new objects could be defined. Einstein's speculation upon the relations of motion to measurement and its units antedates his realization that the Michelson-Morley findings and the Lorentz transformations presented the data for the doctrine of relativity. Quanta, on the other hand, present perceptual findings defined in terms of current theory, yet contradicting it. The approach to the problem may be from either side: from that of the particular experience that controverts the theory, or from that of the developed relational theory that offers new objects to scientific investigation.

If we ask, then, what is the logical or cognitive value of the scientist's realism, we receive two different answers. The one breaks out of his attitude in seeking the solution of the problems with which his research is occupied. The other appears in his metaphysical interpretation of this attitude. In the first we find that the scientist's assumption of the independence of the world in which are found the data of science and the objects a tested theory reveals over against the observation and speculation of the scientist, refers always to the world in so far as it is not involved in the problem upon which he is engaged, and in so far as that world is revealed in scientifically competent, undisputed and tested observation and hypothesis. His acceptance of a real world independent of his processes of knowledge is not based upon the finality of the findings of science, either in its data, or in its logically consistent and experimentally tested theories. Although the data of science, when rigorously ascertained, have a much longer life in the history of science than its theories, they are always possibly subject to revision. This conceivable lack of finality does not, however, affect the data's independence of observation and thought within the field of research. The world to which the data belong is independent of the perception and thought which had failed to recognize them, and any conceivable revision of these data will simply find itself in another world of scientific findings. The scientist has no way of presenting the impermanence of his data except in terms of improved technique, and the same is true of the objects into which the data disappear when a theory has been tested and accepted. They are independent only of the perception and thought of a world whose eyes were as yet closed to them.

The elaborate and highly abstruse relativistic theories carry with them the logical finality of any consistent deduction; but their finality in the history of science depends, first, upon their competent formulation of the independent reality, and, second, upon their success in anticipating later events. And the scientist himself expects this doctrine to be reconstructed just as other scientific doctrines have been reconstructed. He is confident that any later theory will assimilate into its relational structure the data of present-day science—in so far as these stand the test of repetition and improved technique—and the logical structure of present day theories, as relativity has assimilated the logical structure of classical mechanics; but neither his attitude as a research scientist nor his method anticipates the finality of the doctrine. What calls for emphasis is that the independent reality carries with it no implication of finality.

We have seen that this independent reality, which is an essential part of the scientist's apparatus, breaks out at two points. First, in the scientific datum it is an accredited experience which runs counter to interpretations and meanings that have hitherto had their place in the world within which we have been living: for example, the reflections of radiations of dark bodies in the quantum problem. Or it is a new object, relationally defined, a so-called "conceptual" object, in so far as experimental evidence can be given for its existence: for example, the electron, as evidenced in Millikan's oil-drop experiment, or the alpha-particle in Rutherford's photographs. Here is a reality actually there, standing on its own feet in spite of accepted meanings and doctrines that contravene it. Or, in the second place, it is the reality of a new theory justified by unquestioned logical implications and supported by observations and experiments that fulfill its own prophecies. The spear-point of independence is thus always directed against objects or ideas belonging to the very experience within which the scientific datum, or the new theory, has appeared.

In the perspectives of every-day perceptual experience we give directly or inferentially to the distant object—predominantly a visual object—the dimensions it assumes or will assume in a field of common distance and contact experience. The "reality" of a visual object is what one can see himself handling. The visual structure is dominant and even the contact values are ordered in a visual space; but the visual space of immediate proximity to the individual, within which perceptual perspectives have disappeared, lies within a uniform spatial structure coinciding with the grosser structure of contact experience. Contact experience is the "matter" of common-sense, for it is the goal of that mediate experience within which lie all physical objects, which are in advance of the consummations within the physiological act, and which serve, in organisms that are capable of manipulation, as implements for final consummations. But the spatial structure remains visual because of the superior fineness and exactitude of vision. All distant visual experience is symbolic, in Berkeley's sense; but it is symbolic not of pure contact dimensions, but of those exact dimensions which are ordered in the visual space of our radius of manipulation. Final perceptual reality, however, always presupposes actual or possible manipulatory contact, i.e., it presupposes matter.

The conduct of the individual organism does not necessarily involve more than successful organization of distant stimuli into manipulatory responses under the control of the visual field. That is, appropriate conduct with reference to a distant object may take place without the appearance of physical objects in the experience of the organism. For a physical object in experience is not only a spatially distant stimulus to which we respond. It is a thing which acts or may act upon us. This experience of interaction we undoubtedly have primarily in the pressures located in things which we feel and manipulate. The condition for the experience may be found in the pressure of the hands or of other different parts of the body against each other; but the action upon us of the thing from its inside is a fundamental character that cannot be thus accounted for.

What has just been said has two different possible settings; that of the epistemological problem, and that of the development of the infant's immature experience into that of the community to which he belongs. The epistemologist has assumed that all perceptual experience involves awareness, that is, that all of it carries a cognitive reference to a something that is not itself, and his problem is found in the attempted identification of this cognitive reference to a world that lies outside of the experience of the individual with the cognition of the individual that attains its goal within experience. The epistemologist starts, therefore, with the immediate experience of the individual and attempts by way of this cognitive reference to reach a world outside of the individual's experience. The biologist and genetic psychologist, on the other hand, start with the world which the individual enters, and undertake to show how this world fashions the experience of the individual, and how he refashions it. The scientist, of course, is working within the setting of the biologist and the psychologist. In his research he must start with a problem that lies within an unquestioned world of observation and experiment. His problem has thrown into doubt certain features of this world but the scientific data are established in what is not shaken. In so far as the perceptual experience of the individual is inadequate—falls short of objectivity—it must be possible to analyse out of it what is not questioned and can be tested by competent observation and experiment. This observation and experiment imply a perceptual world not lying within the problematic area. For the scientist the problem of knowledge does not arise until the exception appears, or until the logical development of the structure of the world brings with it new objects that call for reconstruction.

But while the scientist must observe, measure and experiment within a perceptual world, the hypotheses of recent years, supported and confirmed by experimental tests, have led to the construction of scientific objects which have invaded the field of the perceptual object, and seem to have made of those objects upon and among which his most accurate measurements are carried out, a problem which his scientific doctrine cannot ignore.

Under the doctrine of the classical mechanics, the perceptual experiences of weight and effort were directly correlated with mass and force. And they were continua which actually or in imagination could be subdivided indefinitely. From the visual-tactual space of what I have termed the manipulatory area, the here and the there, the right and left, and the up and down of perceptual space could be abstracted and there still was left a continuous medium, whose systems of coördinates were subject to arbitrary change of position without affecting the validity of mechanical laws when applied to systems of bodies related to different coördinates. Newtonian absolute space carried with it no incongruity when the physicist made his observations and carried out his experiments in his perceptual world. His own system of coördinates was replaceable by any other without affecting the value of his deductions. Imagination, therefore, carried on indefinitely what the microscope accomplished within its limited range. It presented as perceptual what lay beyond the range of perception, without implying that that which it presented was other than a fractional part of that which was perceptual. Physicists could construct models of their hypotheses that were but the finer anatomy of the perceptual world.

But with the theories of electro-magnetism came an analysis which led to elements which could no longer be fractional parts of perceptual things. Lord Kelvin sought to hold on to them, and stated that he could not understand an hypothesis which he could not present in the form of a model. But the lack of invariance in the Maxwell equations, the transformations of Larmor and Lorentz by which this difficulty was conquered, and Einstein's interpretation of the Lorentz transformations got behind the very structure of the percept. The perceptual thing separates space and time. It is what it is *maugré* time. And if it is subject to time's decay, it is the function of science to get back to those permanent elements which persist. The imperishable atoms of Newton possessed contents of mass which were irrelevant to time. In the perceptual world physical things are the preconditions of events. In the electro-magnetic world the ultimate elements of physical things are events, for time has become an essential characteristic of their contents. Velocities determine mass and dimensions. The outcome, as we have already seen, is a space-time within which events are geometrically plotted, and which should in its geometrical configurations swallow up not only inertial and gravitational energy but also that of electromagnetism, if the program which Einstein has presented, after his initial success in dealing with gravitation, is carried through to its completion.

The scientist finds himself, then, in a perceptual world within which he can make carefully devised observations and refined measurements, the reality of which he does not question in the face of the problem that engages his attention. What he does question are the objects of that world within which contradictions or discrepancies have broken out. Abstraction from these questionable characteristics leaves him still with perceptual objects constituting his scientific data, which moreover will be made the test of any hypothesis that he may advance as a solution of his problem. It is the scientific datum in the world to which it belongs which constitutes for him the independent reality, that reality that is independent of any hypothesis. In so far as he recognizes that a problem may break out anywhere in experience, such data may be said to be independent of any object or structure of objects; but such a problem must arise in a world which will present its own unquestioned scientific data. That is, the scientist never approaches the world as a whole. He must cease to be a research scientist and become a philosopher before the so-called epistemological problem can be his problem.

In the field of classical mechanics his own abstracted space and time could be imaginatively conceived of as indefinitely divisible. They were continua whose fractional parts made up the wholes of this abstracted perceptual space and time. Furthermore there appeared in perceptual experience not only volumes that were continua capable of such divisions, but also contents of pressure and resistance that were also continua capable of like subdivision, and were correlated with the physical concept of mass, both as quantity of matter and as inertia. These contact experiences occupy a critical position in perception, since they present within the manipulatory area what is symbolized in the distance experience. They constitute the "matter" of the physical object promised by our distance experiences. The objects the scientist observes, and the apparatus he handles and with which he makes his most refined measurements, are subject to this test of perceptual reality. The contact experience must answer to the visual experience if the objects and their world are there. The close correlation of mass and motion with the matter of perceptual experience, and that of the continua of the space and time of physical science with those abstracted from perceptual experience, made it possible without friction or incongruity to present the scientific objects of classical mechanics in the perceptual field of the scientist's own scientific data.

I have already referred to the profound revolution in the conception of the physical object which the theories of electro-magnetism and relativity have brought about. The perceptual object must be there in order that it may endure. The perceptual object cannot be an event. Events in the perceptual world presuppose physical things that have locations, and material contents that are irrelevant to time. In the structure of the perceptual world space and time are inevitably separated. A world of space-time occupied by events is no longer congruous with the perceptual world, and the only correlation between the two is that of logical patterns. The world of the scientist's experimental findings cannot belong to the world to which they refer.

And there is another revolutionary phase in this most modern physical theory. While all of our distance experience—predominantly the world of vision—points to a reality of contact, though this is placed and ordered in a structure in which eye and hand mutually control each other; the universe of relativity is entirely visual, fashioned by the mechanism of light signals. These signals, immediately directed toward physical things, are reflected from one consentient set to another, so that their reality is never found in any moving or resting thing but rather in transformation-formulae by which one distance structure may be translated into another; while the ultimate space-time to which they are referred is a texture that is so caught in its own curvature that these distance symbols can only symbolize the logic of symbolization. It is as though the possibility of formulating any set of meanings in terms of any other set of meanings were used to reduce all meanings to the mechanism of translation. Matter transferred to distance experience becomes only a curvature of space-time.

I have already touched upon that character of the physical thing which exhibits itself in its acting upon us and other physical things from within itself, from its inside. This character does not appear in the scientist's account of physical things. His statement of inertia as the tendency of a body to remain in the state of rest or motion in which it is found, and of force as that which is the cause of such a state, is always in terms of velocities, accelerations, decelerations, and their ratios to each other. It never deals with the inside of a body but only with the outside which the analysis of the body reveals.

It is a matter of course that the things involved in the observation of the scientist, and the apparatus of his laboratory and experiment are not part of the uncertain field of his problem, and that they have a reality independent of the solution of the problem. Otherwise the problem could never be solved. For example, the actual observations of the position of the stars about the eclipsed sun upon the negatives and the apparatus by which these positions were measured to high degrees of accuracy, unquestionably had a reality to the scientist upon which he depended for his judgment of Einstein's hypothesis. His ultimate reality is found in these carefully devised observations and experiments, and the things there present do not fall under doubt—at least until a new problem arises which may involve these very things and the scientist's experience of them. Then, however, he approaches the new problem with a set of equally carefully devised observations and experiments and the unquestioned things which these involve.

It is also true that at the other end of his undertaking when he has assured himself of the viability of his hypothesis, and has perhaps stated it with the finality of the geometry of a Minkowski space-time, this finality in form has no place in his scientific attitude. He is as ready to find a problem within this system as elsewhere in the universe. His finality of statement is logical, that is, it is an affirmation that the hypothesis has been brought into consistent relation to all other pertinent findings in the world as it exists for us. For the moment it meets the demands of what we call the facts, as for example the Newtonian mechanics did for two centuries. Both the factual setting of his problem and the successful *dénouement* of his investigation have in the scientist's world a reality that belongs to the present, without the slightest prejudgment as to their reality in a later present. It is only when he philosophizes that the relation of these presents to each other becomes a problem. It is not and cannot be a scientific problem, for it could neither be stated nor solved by an experimental method.

If we recur to the reality of the data in the scientist's procedure, we recognize, as I have already noted, that the data have in one sense a longer period than the objects in terms of which they are stated. In the case of photographs of the positions of the stars about the rim of the eclipsed sun, these positions are stated in terms of the changes in chemical structures on the plate. The nature of these chemical structures, and what takes place under exposure to light, will probably change with the development of physical science; but the relative positions of these spots on the plate will remain unaffected by the different nature of the plate as an object. In the same fashion relative positions of the stars and planets can be traced in reports of the observations of Mesopotamian astrologers, in the catalogues of Grecian astronomers, in the recorded observations of Tycho Brahe, and in those of Copernican astronomers. The objects these various watchers of the sky saw were profoundly different, but it is possible to identify in all these records the same relative positions. It would, however, be a mistake to assume that the scientist could observe simply relative positions, or that in the world of reality by which he tests hypotheses such abstractions can have an independent existence. They are abstractions from things and have reality only in the concretion of these things. The scientist may or may not be uncertain of the nature of the stars, but if his uncertainty were resolved, the stars would be objects in his perceptual world whose positions he would be recording, though the stars will presumably have another nature for later astronomers. Furthermore even in his uncertainty he must be observing unquestioned perceptual objects—distant spots of light and photographic plates. A world cannot be constructed from scientific data that have been abstracted from the world within which the problem arises. It is also true that in testing the logical consistency of his theory the scientist carries his problem back, at least presumptively, into the structure of those perceptual objects that his problem does not affect, but if such objects lie outside the problem, any inconsistency militates against the theory, not against the reality of the objects.

Now the import of this character of the scientist's method is, as Professor Dewey has long since insisted, that the knowledge-process lies inside of experience, and that the so-called percepts that have not fallen under the doubt knowledge seeks to resolve are simply there, and are affected with no cognitive character. We are not aware of objects about us, except as we seek to reassure ourselves of their existence, their qualities and their meanings; though any object may fall under suspicion and so become an assured object of knowledge. We must be able, for logical and methodological purposes, to state things which are simply there in terms of what we do find in our cognitive adventures.

I will not argue at length Professor Dewey's analysis of cognition, since I am not likely to better his account of it, nor make it more convincing to those whom he has not convinced. I should, however, like to emphasize one feature of this experience which is called perception even when it is applied to what is simply there apart from any attitude of awareness on the part of the so-called percipients. This feature is that of the distance-character of all our perceptual objects. As I have already indicated, this experience is one which is dominated by the head and its neural inheritance.

The physical thing has arisen in experience through the direct control of our conduct toward it in so far as it is related to our organisms by the distance senses lodged in the head, when this relation through the distance-senses calls out in advance and controls manipulatory reactions toward the distant object we are seeking or avoiding. The perceptual object answers to a collapsed act, and if we are in doubt as to the reality of what we see or hear, we must carry the act out to the point of actual contact. The doubting Thomas can be convinced only by his hand. Even tactual illusion can only be dissipated by other contacts. The world that stretches away from our manipulatory area, especially in its perspective characters, is most readily thrown into the cognitive field, though this never concerns more than certain features of the world. There is always a world of perceptual reality there which is the basis for our investigation. It is easy therefore for the psychologist and the epistemologist with his penny to generalize this attitude and attach awareness to all perceptual experience. The answer to him is to be found in the location of his doubt and the fashion in which he dispels it.

We cannot, of course, go back of the immediate experience of handling or seeing an object. But we can state the conditions under which the object of our manipulation and sight is there. These conditions include not only the structure of the physical world in which the objects are found, but also the organism which is related to it and to them. In this sense we can follow out the reflected light as it travels to the retina and the passage of the nervous excitation as it travels along the optic nerve to the central tracts; and in the same fashion we can follow out the excitation of the nerves which pass from the skin, muscles and joints in our handling of the object.

But it is evident that this analysis takes place within a

world of things not thus analysed; for the objects about us are unitary objects, not simple sums of the parts into which analysis would resolve them. And they are what they are in relation to organisms whose environment they constitute. When we reduce a thing to parts we have destroyed the thing that was there. It is no longer a table or a tree or an animal. And even if by some process these parts should coalesce and become the things that they were, it still remains the case that they would not be things they were in this environment of this organism, if they ceased to be parts of this environment. We refer to these differences as the meanings these things have in their relationship to the organisms. Still, these meanings belong to the things, and are as objective as are those characters of the things that belong to them in the environments of other organisms. The sensuous characters are largely the same for organisms endowed with like apparatus of sense perception; though there are always differences in these characters due to differences in these apparatuses and to the conditions under which the things enter into relation with the senses of the various organisms. Other characters such as nutritiousness for an animal that can digest and assimilate certain things, dangerousness or protection, equally arise as objective characters when the objects enter relations with certain organisms, and take on these meanings. Such characters evidently emerge with the development of organisms and in their changing experience.

Science undertakes to isolate the conditions under which these new things arise, or have arisen. It abstracts from the peculiarities of particular experience and seeks that which is common among as many experiences as possible. It thus reaches things which upon the supposition of analysis have a common reality apart from the particular experience within which the analysed objects existed. We thus reach things that belong to any possible experience up to the limits of our powers of generalization. The question arises whether that which answers to these widest generalizations escapes from experience, and from the characters and meanings which belong to experience. Can we in thought reach that which is independent of the situation within which the thinking takes place? I am asking the question not from the standpoint of the metaphysician and logician, who start with an apparatus of thinking and a cognition that are preconditions of the experience within which they appear; but from the standpoint of a science that has undertaken to trace the development of thought out of the lowliest types of behavior. If we posit a mind having an inherent power of entering into cognitive relation with objects that are simply there for its awareness and thought, this mind may be able to identify things independent of the experiences of the organisms that have become in some fashion endowed with such minds. Or we may with the idealists transfer all environments to mind itself. But if mind is simply an emergent character of certain organisms in their so-called intelligent responses to their environments, mind can never transcend the environment within which it operates. Nor can it by generalizing all possible experiences get beyond any possible experience; for it must do its thinking within some experience, and the meanings that arise out of the relation of the minded organism to its environment must belong to the object of its perception and its widest thought. It may be claimed that an emergent evolution can not deny the possibility of the emergence of a realist's mind, with just that power of entering into cognitive relations with objects; the answer, however, will be found in the natural history of mind and the study of mental operations.

II

The Physical Thing[1]

A. It is evident that a definition of the physical thing in terms of manipulatory and distance experience must apply also to the organism as a physical thing. The organism is seen and felt. We supplement what comes through direct vision by what is obtained through mirrors and visual images, and our hands come into contact with practically the whole surface of our bodies. Kinaesthetic and visceral experiences can be located as inside our organisms only when these organisms have attained outsides. If we use pressures of surfaces of our own bodies against each other in the experience of bodies acting upon us, this only takes place in so far as the body and other objects have been organized in a common field of physical things. Without doubt surfaces in contact and organic experiences bounded by these surfaces are, in the experience of the infant, the experiences out of which the outsides and insides of things arise. However, the child can delimit his bodily surfaces only through things not his body, and he reaches the entire surfaces of things not his body before he reaches his own organism as a bounded thing. Genetically the infant advances from the periphery toward his body. If he uses the pressures of the organism in putting insides into things, the body must earlier have been defined by its contacts with bounded things. It is important to recognize that this continues in experience to be the relationship between physical things and the body as a physical thing, and between physical

[1] Sections (A) and (B) in this Essay are parallel accounts taken from two different manuscripts.

things other than the body. We get by analysis into the insides of things only by reaching new outsides which are actually or imaginatively the conditions for that pressure experience which appears as the inside either of the body or of other physical things.

Sets of physical things are then defined by their boundaries, and among those things the bodily organism obtains its definition in the same fashion. If for example we regard the colors and tactual feel of things as dependent upon physiological processes within the organism, the argument proceeds upon the assumption of definable physical things including the organism as there. In experience there is no priority of reality ascribed to the bodily organism. If it is conceivable that the hand should pass through the table that is seen, it is equally conceivable that the hand should pass through the seen leg. These physical things are all of them distance experiences. That is, they are placed in a space, and to be so placed they are ordered from center O of a system of coördinates. The forms in which they appear are optical perspectives, and perception realizes them in terms of the experience of the manipulatory area, in which they are subject to the test of contact, for their perceptual reality; but they remain in that area visual objects. Within this manipulatory area the distortions of the optical perspectives disappear. Things reach standard sizes. That they have standard sizes implies that the center O may be found at any point where the things would have the spatial values found in this manipulatory area. The fundamental postulate of Newtonian physics that any set of Cartesian coördinates may be taken as the basis for the ordering and measuring of things and their motions is involved in our perceptual world. Conceptual thought has formulated logically the attitude of perceptual experience. The question then arises, what is the nature of this attitude by which perception shifts indifferently from one center O to another?

In immediate perception distance stimulations are adequate to call out approach or withdrawal, and consequent contacts and consummations. That perception should present distant objects as having the physical values of the manipulatory area is not involved in the successful behavior of a percipient organism. To say that the memory image of the distant stimulation as it appeared in a manipulatory area is fused with the distant stimulation is to cover up a process with a term. It can be so fused because the distant stimulation is already a physical thing. Within the manipulatory area the object acts upon the percipient organism, and action in the perceptual experience means the pressure of its volume upon the organism. There are an infinity of other characteristics of its action, its temperature, its odor and so forth; but these are all characteristics of it as a massive thing, and this inner nature of the physical thing we never reach by subdividing its visual boundaries. There appears in the physical thing a content which originally belongs only to the organism, that of pressure, what Whitehead has called the "pushiness" of things, and the question is how it gets into the thing. Distant visual and contact tactual boundaries are there in immediate experience. I am not considering the metaphysical question of how we get from an inner experience to a world outside ourselves, but how distant and bounded objects get the insides of perceptual objects—insides never revealed by subdivision. The suggestion which I have already made is that the pressures of bodily surfaces against each other, preëminently of one hand against the other, are transferred to the object, and the question I am raising is how this transference takes place.

The only answer that I can give to the question is that the organism in grasping and pushing things is identifying its own effort with the contact experience of the thing. It increases that experience by its own efforts. To take hold of a hard object is to stimulate oneself to exert that inner effort. One arouses in himself an action which comes also from the inside of the thing. It comes from the inside of the thing because the experience is increased by the action of bodies upon organisms and upon other things within the perceptual world. The organism's object arouses in the organism the action of the object upon the organism, and so becomes endowed with that inner nature of pressure which constitutes the inside of the physical thing. It is only in so far as the organism thus takes the attitude of the thing that the thing acquires such an inside.

The formula for this process is that the thing stimulates the organism to act as the thing acts upon the organism, and that the action of the thing is the organism's resistance to pressure such as arises when a hard object is firmly grasped in the hand. The resistance of the object is continuous with the effort of the hand. In the development of the infant this experience must come earlier than that of its own physical organism as a whole. The infant must be placing this effort of his inside of things before he is in a position to identify the effort as his own. His surroundings stretch away on all sides, and colored shapes come to be located and familiar in a world within which his body comes finally to occupy a defined place. Meantime the pressure of his body and the grasping of his hands have to localize things from an inside attitude, and he finally reaches himself as a thing through the action of other things upon him. Matter is the name we give to this nature of things, and its characteristic is that it is identical with the response that it calls out. Weight as pressure, or inertia as resistance to change of rest or motion, is identical with the effort by which the weight is upheld or the body is brought into motion or set at rest. The body has an abundance of other characters which inhere in the matter, but none of these others has this characteristic. Color, sound, taste, and odor cannot be identified with the responses which they elicit, either in organisms or in other objects; while the experiential inner content of matter is identical with the responses which it calls out in things. It was the striking achievement of Renaissance science that it isolated this character of matter as inertia. Newton could refer to it either as the quantity of matter or as the property of matter by which it continues in its state of rest or motion unless acted upon by an external force. Inertia and force could then be equated. In the equations of Newtonian mechanics mass is defined in terms of force and force is defined in terms of mass. Here Newton was reflecting a fundamental attitude of experience toward things.

We are now, I think, in a position to answer the question raised earlier: how do we come to give to the thing at a distance the physical values of the manipulatory area? Another phrasing of the question would be; what is the experiential background of the homogeneity of space? In the first place, the continuity of the experience of effort and the matter of the physical thing provide a common inner nature of things that is recognized whenever the distance experience is completed in its contact implications. In the second place, this inner nature is there only in so far as it calls out the response of effort. The distant object, setting in train the responses of grasping and manipulation, calls out in the organism its own inner nature of resistance. We have here the basis for Lipps' empathy. It would be a mistake to regard this inner nature of matter as a projection by the organism of its sense of effort into the object. The resistance is in the thing as much as the effort is in the organism, but the resistance is there only over against effort or the action of other things. Brought thus within the field of effort, action and reaction are equal. The inner character of the thing is indeed due to the organism—to the continuity of effort and resistance. However, the character of innerness arises only with the appearance of the organism as an object, with the definition of surfaces and experiences of the organism that lie inside of its bounded surfaces. What I wish to emphasize is that the physical thing in contact pressures, and at a distance in awakening anticipatory manipulatory responses, calls out in the organism what is continuous with its own inner nature, so that the action of the thing where it is, is identified with the response of the organism. It is this that makes it possible for the organism to place itself and its manipulatory area at any distant object, and to extend the space of the manipulatory area indefinitely, thus reaching out of dissonant perspectives a homogeneous space. What is essential is that the physical thing arouses in the organism its own response of resistance, that the organism as matter is acting as the physical thing acts.

There are two expressions I have used above which call for further comment. One is the identification of the inner effort of the organism with the matter of the object. As I have indicated, this does not imply that the organism projects an inner content into the object. The resistance is there over against the effort, but in the organism of the infant there is not only the response of pressing against the thing, but also, through the integration of the central nervous system, the arousal of the response of pressing the other hand against the hand that is pressing the thing. The organism acts upon itself, and in acting upon itself its responses are identical with those it makes to things. The thing, then, arouses in the organism the tendency to respond as the thing responds to the organism. We have learned in recent years that it is the function of the central nervous system in the higher forms to connect every response potentially with every other response in the organism. In a sense all responses are so interconnected by way of interrelated innervation and inhibition. There is a distinction to be made, however, between the object in the manipulatory area that is both seen and handled, and the distant object that is both out of reach and also lies in a visual perspective. We have seen that the continuity of effort and the resistance of matter facilitate the placing of the organism with its manipulatory area at the distant object. The sense in which this takes place is found in the responses which would arise at that location,—responses which are aroused, though inhibited, within the organism. What I have just been indicating is that the distant object calls out the response of its own resistance as well as the effort of reacting to it. What is involved in a distant object being "there" is not simply the tendency to respond to it, even in an anticipatory fashion, nor is its location as a physical object achieved by a mere sensory image of its feel, unless we mean by the memory image the tendency in the infant's organism to press as the distant object presses, thus calling out the tendency to respond with his own pressure. It is this latter response that in our experience constitutes the physical object—a something with an inside. I am convinced that this embodiment of the object in the responses of the organism is the essential factor in the emergence of the physical thing.

The object is there in its immediate resistance to the effort of the organism. It is not there as an object, however, that is, it has no inside. It gets its inside when it arouses in the organism its own response and thus the answering response of the organism to this resistance. What has been termed this nature of the object as it is called out in the organism appears in the sensation of hardness or resistance. There is indeed, as Locke assumed, the same extended resistant nature in the experience of the individual as in the world, but for Locke this was in the experience of the individual an "idea," that is, a sensation. If we recognize the identity of resistance and effort, then the character of an "idea," i.e., something that belongs in the experience of the individual, comes to it when the response of the organism is aroused in the form of the resistance, the inner nature of the thing. These are, as we have seen, identical in character. Both the physical object and the organism are material. What must be shown is that the object arouses in the organism not only an organic response to the physical thing but also a response to itself as an object calling out this response. The mechanism by which this is accomplished is the cerebrum. The mechanism of the cord and its bulb is one simply of responses to outer stimuli. Such stimuli are imperative in their demands. The cerebrum, on the other hand, is an organ which integrates a vast variety of responses, including the lower reflexes, and is specifically the center for the distance sense organs located in the head. In the integrative process there are different alternative combinations and corresponding alternatives also for the inhibitions that integration necessarily involves. This introduces delay in response, and adjustment by way of selection of type of response, i.e., choice. Choice implies more than the contest of two or more stimuli for the control of the organic response. It implies that the situation is in some sense within the behavior pattern in the organism. What is not done defines the object in the form in which we do react to it. The bounding surfaces of an object, its resistances in various possible reactions upon it, the uses to which it could be put in varying degrees, go to make up that object, and are characters of the object that would lose their static nature if the responses they involve were actually carried out.

They are competitors for the action of the organism, but in so far as they are not carried out they constitute the object upon which the action takes place, and within the whole act fix the conditions of the form the act takes on. All these responses are found in the nervous system as paths of reaction interconnected with all the other paths. If certain responses are prepotent they *ipso facto* inhibit all the others. It is possible to follow this process of inhibition in some detail in the use of antagonistic muscles and conflicting reflexes. There is as definite a relaxation of certain muscles as there is innervation of others. In order to carry out one response, the cerebrum inhibits other responses. The system is as responsible for what it does not do as for what it does.

Within the field of matter, the resistance which the volume of a body offers to the hand, or to any surface of the body, and the tendencies to manipulate it when seen at a distance, are organized in various ways. There is, for example, the tendency to pick up a book on a distant table. The form and resistance of the book are present in some sense in the adjustment already present in the organism when the book is seen. My thesis is that the inhibited contact responses in the distance experience constitute the meaning of the resistance of the physical object. They are, in the first place, in opposition to the responses actually innervated or in prospect of being innervated. They are competitors for the field of response. They also within the whole act fix the conditions of the actual response. I am referring specifically to the responses which go to make up matter in the distance experience. If I see a distant book an indefinite number of manipulatory responses are aroused, such as grasping it in a number of ways, opening, tearing its leaves, pressing upon it, rubbing it, and a host of others. One, picking up the book, is prepotent and organizes the whole act. It therefore inhibits all others. The tendencies to perform these others involve the same resistance of manipulation, and are now in direct opposition to the prepotent response; but while in opposition they provide the conditions for the exercise of the prepotent response. The feel of the book if one rubbed it, the contours if one passed one's hands about it, the possibility of opening the book, etc., determine the form that the grasping and lifting up of the book will take. In general what one does not do to the book, in so far as this calls out the same resistance as that given in actually manipulating the book, and in so far as it is inhibited by what one does do to the book, occupies in the experience the "what the book is" over against the response which is the expression of the act. Inhibition here does not connote bare nonexistence of these responses, for they react back upon the prepotent response to determine its form and nature. The way in which one grasps the book is determined by the other paths of response, both by those that are inhibited and by the controls of adjustments in which responses not carried out are yet partially innervated. The act is a moving balance within which many responses play in and out of the prepotent response. What is not done acts in continual definition of what is done. It is the resistance in what is not done that is the matter of the object to which we respond.

So far as the world exists for the organism, so far as it is the environment of the organism, it is reflected in the reactions of the organism to the world. What we actually come into contact with is there over against the organism, but by far the larger part of what surrounds us we do not rest upon nor manipulate. It is distant from us in space and in time; yet it has an inner content that is a continuation of what lies under our feet and within our grasp. These distant objects not only call out in us direct responses of moving toward or away from and manipulating them, but they also arouse in us the objects that act upon us from within ourselves. I have been seeking to present the neural mechanism by which this inner nature of the outside thing appears in experience.

If the sight of the book calls out a direct response of movement toward it, there is in this response nothing but the excitement of the organism to that act. If, however, all the other responses the book may be responsible for, are aroused, they can only enter into the act in so far as they are inhibited or coördinated. They are in opposition to the prepotent response of moving toward the book until the integration of the act arranges them in their spatial and temporal relations with the inhibition of their immediate expression. It is this opposition which I have referred to as resistance. The brain is the portion of the central nervous system that belongs to the distance senses. It has, however, direct connection with the reflexes of the spinal system. It not only orients the head, and so the organism, toward distant objects, but also connects these distant stimuli with the responses of the trunk and the limbs which these objects call out when the organism has been brought into contact range of the objects, so that these later responses are aroused in advance of the situation within which they can be effectively innervated. The object is then expressing itself in the organism not only in stimulating it to approach or withdrawal but also in arousing in anticipatory fashion reactions that will later be carried out. By the term "expresses itself" I mean that the relations that make of the surrounding objects the environment of the organisms are active in the organism. The environment is there for the organism in the interrelationship of organism and environment. The delayed responses integrated in the act toward the distant object constitute the object as it will be or at least may be for the organism. But that it may be an object it must have an inner content, which we refer to as the results of responses now delayed. That these should be in some sense present in the distant object is what calls for explanation. The explanation I am offering is in terms of the resistance they meet in the prepotent act with reference to which they must be integrated. This resistance is found in the adjustment and delay in execution and the inhibitions these entail.

The primary phase of this resistance we have found to lie in the matter of the physical object. The continuity of the resistance of the object with the resistances of parts of the organism to each other constitutes the matter both of the objects and of the organism, and carries over to objects the innerness of organic resistances to them, while the objects in their spatial organization lead to the definition of the organism as a physical object. But, as I have already noted, this resistance appears as the innerness of the physical thing only when the object calls out in the organism the object's own attitude of resistance. The physical thing uses our tendencies to resist in advance of actual contact, so that it exists in the behavior of the organism, not as the organism's sensation, but as the entrance of the organism into objects, through its assuming their attitudes and thus defining and controlling its own response. There is, of course, the immediate response of the organism to the pressure that comes upon it, into which the object as object does not enter. Here there is no character of an object which would be denominated as a sensation. There is merely the brute response of organism to its environment. But when this attitude of resistance of the object to the organism can be aroused within the organism itself, over against the organism's resistance to it, then there is that which a philosophy of mind could locate in the organism as mental—an idea, in Locke's sense. An examination of the growth of the infant's experience, however, shows that the environment must first have entered the organic responses of the child as a resistance it possesses in common with resistances which the organism offers to itself, before the organism could define itself and its experiences over against the physical things around it. It is the mechanism of the cerebrum which, in its connections with the responses of the cord and the brain stem, has made possible this playing the part of the physical object within the behavior of the organism; and in particular it has utilized the manipulatory responses of the hand in their interruption of the procedure of the response to its consummation. Here the common resistance of thing and hand opens the door to the thing to play its part in the behavior of the organism. And it remained for Renaissance science to isolate these measurable characteristics of the physical thing, as the conditions for all other characters of the thing as they appear in experience.

In immediate experience the thing is smooth or rough, is pleasant or painful, as directly as it is resistant. Smoothness or roughness or pleasantness or distress involve various responses carried out toward the distant object, and these enter into the organization of the act even though immediately inhibited. That they are not immediately carried out means that they are organized about the prepotent response of approach or withdrawal and subsequent reactions. My thesis is that the resistance which this organization of the act puts upon them identifies them as characters of the thing, though as qualities which inhere in the physical thing as a resistant object. The surface we call smooth calls out a tendency to stroke it, but that one may not do this until he has reached it and got hold of it means that the actual appearance of smoothness or pleasantness awaits the manipulatory resistance of the physical thing. The dependence of the appearance of these characters upon the act organized with reference to the attainment of the physical object is the organic phase of the contact reality of the distance object. My point is that this contact reality of the distance object asserts itself in neural organization by the inhibition of the reaction which these characters of the distant object call out through the organized act which realizes them. In so far as the tendency to stroke the distant smooth object is held in check by the organization of the act which will realize the tendency, it is an affirmation of the conditional reality of the smoothness of the object. If it cannot fit into the organization of such an act we dismiss it as illusory; e.g., the apparent wetness of the shimmer above the desert sand cannot be fitted into the act of going to and drinking the illusory water. It is the acceptance of inhibitions involved in the organized attitude of approach that confers these qualities upon the distant object. The resistances involved in organization lead up to processes that are aroused before they can be realized and which yet can determine the form of the act which completes them.

The development of the head, and of the cerebrum as the seat of the distance senses, has given to the organism the two fundamental characters that belong to mind. It has brought about the anticipatory arousal of reactions that can only be realized upon the accomplishment of the reaction of the body to its immediate resistances in reaching its goal. In the organization of the act so that these aroused but uncompleted reactions may be fulfilled it has introduced the future into the mechanism of the act, and the conditioning of the present and future by each other. Again, it has made possible the excitement within the organism of that resistance of the physical thing which is common to thing and organism. The physical thing external to the organism can call out its own response and the answering reaction of the organism. In the form of spatially defined resistance the action of the distant object is present in the responses of the organism, with its value in exciting the appropriate reactions of the organism. In the form of a response the distant object is present in the conduct of the organism. Furthermore, other characters of the object, dependent for their realization upon the carrying out of an organic act, become, through the organization of the responses to them into the act and the acceptance of its control, ways in which the object appears in the conduct of the organism. The object can thus appear in experience through the reaction of the organism to it, given the mechanism of the upper nervous system. It is there in the values it will have, reflected in the responses of the organism; but it is there in advance of the responses. And it is because the objects are there that the organism can become an object itself in its experience.

B. There is a characteristic difference between the so-called primary and the secondary qualities. The stuff of matter appears in the primary qualities of extension, effective occupation of space and mobility. These answer in our experience to what has been called by Newton the quantity of matter. This appears in immediate experience of the spatial resistance of the body. It appears in momentum. At least this is experience of the object as offering extended resistance, of our own bodies acquiring momentum, of the effort necessary to set a massive body in motion and to change its state of motion. Extension, volume, and resistance to change of rest or motion, these cannot be exactly defined in terms of our sensuous experience, but they are characters which enable us to put ourselves inside of the physical object. Its resistance is equal to ours. It feels the same. In the case of the secondary qualities the characters which appear in our vision, hearing, tasting and smelling cannot be shared with the characters in the physical object which they answer to. It is not by being red, or salt, or noisy, or redolent that the organism finds itself in relation with objects having these characters. It is by resisting that the organism is in relationship with resistant objects. If we seek for the biological mechanism of this experience, as we do for that of the other so-called senses, we find it in the resistances which the different parts of the organism present to each other. The hand, notably, presses against different parts of the body, and they, in response to that pressure, resist it. When one presses against the surface of a table he has the same experience as when he presses against his hand, except for the absence of the response of resisting the pressure of the other hand. But there is a common content there, by means of which the organism later passes over into the insides of things. In no other sensuous experience do we pass over into the thing. It can affect us by its color, odor, flavor or temperature, but the relation does not set up in us the character of the object. Resistance, or the effective occupation of space, Locke's "solidity," has in experience a common character, as Locke felt, which is both in the individual and in outer things. If we state it in terms of an "idea," of a sensation in the mind, the whole affair, external effect as well as internal feeling, is shut up in the mind, where Berkeley placed it, and where Hume left it to be dispersed with the other impressions of the mind. What calls for further analysis than the psychology of their period admitted is that phase of the physical thing which I have referred to as its inside. This term does not refer to the new surfaces discovered by subdivision of the thing. It does involve that unity of the thing which Kant and his idealistic followers located in the judging process; but it involves more than this—viz., an element of activity, expressed in the term *resistance*. When one hand presses against the other, each hand resists the other from the inside. As I have said, when the hand presses against a table there is an element in the resistance of the table that is identical with what we find in the mutual resistance of the two hands; but while the table resists the hand as effectually as does the other hand, the resistance of the table, taken as an abstracted experience, lacks the character of activity that belongs to the pressure of the opposing hand. Yet it requires an abstraction to take this character out of the table. To say that we put this character into the thing, whose mass or inertia resists forces acting upon it, means either going back to a doctrine of consciousness of stuff which separates the individual from physical things rather than interrelates him with them, or else it ignores the fact that the individual's organism comes into experience only as other objects define and orient it. Nor are we justified in assuming that an individual locates an inside within himself before he does in other things. It ought to be sufficiently evident, though it is in fact quite generally overlooked, that we become physical things no sooner than do the objects that surround us, and that we anatomize ourselves, as Russell has recently pointed out, only as we anatomize others. But it is possible to recognize in the evolution of the neo-pallium a mechanism by which higher organisms can live in an environment occupied by physical things, including themselves, all of which have insides. Undoubtedly a response from an inside must come from the organism and not from the physical thing outside it, but it cannot be located within the organism until the organism has been defined by its interrelations with other things.

What the extensive development of the cerebrum has made possible is the innervation and organization of responses in advance of their execution. When an organism endowed with such organs finds its hand pressing against a resistant object, there will be an experience common to the pressure of the object and of the other hand, and there will be also a stimulus to respond with answering pressure just as the other hand would respond. The organism has stimulated itself, by its action on an object, to act upon itself in the fashion of the other object. To an animal whose central nervous system includes only a spinal column and a brain stem, whose responses, therefore, take place without delay, such a tendency to react to its own reaction to an object would be incongruous and meaningless. To an animal, whose exteroceptors put it into relation with the object from afar, and whose neo-pallium enables it to start and organize its responses in advance of satisfying or dangerous contact, it is of immense advantage to be able to act in a manner in the place of the distant object and thus to be ready for its own subsequent reaction. Where the action of other things upon us is in some degree identical with responses of our own, so that the beginning of our action upon them can stimulate us to call out in our organisms delayed response that puts us in their attitudes, they can become objects to us at the same time that we can become objects to ourselves, since we are approaching our own later action from the point of view of the other. For we can never become selves unless the action in which we are involved includes action toward our own organisms. Undoubtedly to become conscious selves the mechanism of communication is necessary, but the matrix for communication is the stimulation we give to ourselves to act as those upon whom we are acting will act.

There are then two characters of the physical thing, if we regard it from the standpoint of the genesis of experience as we find it in the individual, and as we infer it to have taken place in the early history of the human community. The first character is that of the continuity of the experience of pressure in the organism and of resistance in the physical object. The experience of the organism in its contact with the physical object is the pressure which is the character of the physical object. This, as we have seen, distinguishes the contact experience from the experiences of so-called secondary qualities. What is experienced is the resistance of the physical thing, and the experience of this resistance is itself resistance in the organism. As the expression, "experience of," carries with it dangerous implications it is better to state the proposition in this manner: that in contact experience the resistant character of the object is identical with the resistant character of the organism; while in distance experience the character of the object is in no way present in the organism. The second character the object undoubtedly borrows from the organism, in becoming an object, that of actually or potentially acting upon the organism from within itself. I have also called this character that of "having an inside." It is the character of resistance identical in the organism and in the object that opens the door to this borrowing. To take the attitude of pressing against an object is to arouse in the organism the attitude of counter-pressure. This is a fundamental attitude reflected also in Newton's law of action and reaction. There must be an action of the object equal to the action of the organism upon it, in order that it may be in our experience a physical thing. In grasping the object, in pushing it, in leaning against it, in any manipulation of it, the object must come back upon the organism with equal resistance, if it is to be and maintain itself as a thing. Psychological analysis has here used the term "kinaesthetic imagery," and aesthetic analysis has referred to it as "empathy." We see the object not simply as offering passive resistance, but as actively resisting us. But the fundamental importance of these facts for the emergence of the physical object in experience has not, I think, been recognized. It is easily overlooked, because the attitude of the thing's response to pressure is identical with that of the organism, though opposite in direction. This opposition reveals itself in the appearance of the organism as a physical object. Such an object can only appear when the organism has taken the attitude of acting toward itself, and the invitation to this is found in the fact that we have stimulated ourselves by our attitude toward the physical thing to respond in pressure as the thing responds.

There are two matters to be considered here. One is the relatively late abstraction of the physical object from the social object and the necessity that the organism take the attitude of the other in order to become an object to himself. The other is the structure of space in our experience. This finds its expression in the Cartesian coördinates and in the preservation of the identical structure no matter where the origin of the system is placed. It is the first item in Newtonian relativity. In our perceptual space an individual finds the center of the system within himself, and the coordinates extend up and down, to right and left and before and behind him. They are organically given in his bilateral symmetry and his maintenance of his erect position over against a distant object in the line of vision. What I wish to point out is that perceptual space involves something more than this orientation. Distortions of distant visual space are corrected in perception to a very considerable degree. We see things in the dimensions and structure of the manipulatory area. That is, we extend to them the space of the manipulatory area. Now evidently this can only be accomplished in immediate experience if there is in perception a mechanism for taking the attitude of the distant object. It is the sight of the distant physical thing that stimulates the organism to take its attitude of resistance, which is the import of seeing a hard thing. The sight of a physical thing anywhere in our field of perception locates us there as well as where we are, and, indeed, because it locates us where we are. Over and above the tendency to move toward or away from the distant object, immediate location in perceptual space implies the presence of a thing at the point, and the presence of a thing beyond the stimulation to approach or move away involves the character of action of the thing at the point—its active resistance, borrowed, as I have said, from the responses of the organism.

III

Scientific Objects and Experience

The knowledge process takes a different route for the scientist from that which it takes for the epistemologist. The scientist starts with an unquestioned material world and with unquestioned objects that appear in the problem with which his research is occupied; from these he proceeds by inference to the formulation of his hypothesis and the consequences which it involves, and then on to the observation and experiment by which his hypothesis is tested. Although he criticizes his perceptual experiences and exhibits the errors and illusions of perception, his criticism is always founded on objects that are there; and his criticism does not invalidate these, since he must appeal to them as tests of the errors he discovers. In the process of thinking out the hypothesis his ideas symbolize relations in a world that is there, and he tentatively seeks to find among them such interrelations as will overcome conflicts between objects and their meanings, or between different meanings of things. He finally deduces the results that follow from his hypothetical reconstruction, and by observation and experiment in an unquestioned world finds, or fails to find, the confirmation he is seeking. His cognitive proceeding is from an accepted perceptual world through exceptional instances and conflicting meanings on to the same world, after its meanings have been reconstructed. That world itself he never questions.

The epistemologist, on the other hand, proceeds from the fact that all perceptual experiences are dependent upon the relation of the world to the organism, and makes use of such experiences as illusions and perceptual errors in order to locate percepts in a consciousness entirely separate from the world of objects to which these percepts refer. This position was strongly fortified by the doctrine of Renaissance science that secondary qualities cannot belong to the physical world with which physical science is occupied. Knowledge, as the epistemologist conceives it, undertakes to proceed from these states of consciousness, including all perceptual experience, over to an ontologically separate world to which these states of consciousness seem to refer. He is thus led to the conclusion that a cognitive reference attaches to all perceptual experience. The existence of a world to which such states of consciousness refer becomes the epistemologist's problem.

It is important to place the scientific object in its relation to the perceptual world, which is, as we have seen, presupposed both in the scientist's problem and in his experimental data. That object is an abstraction of that within experience which is subject to exact measurement. It is furthermore a physical thing, i.e., it occupies a volume of extension that could conceivably be brought within the range of a manipulatory experience. Even when we pursue de Broglie's idea and state matter in terms of wave motion, we must come back to a definable portion of space which is in so far within our field of conceivable manipulation that we could measure the waves. The ether, as long as science retained it, could be conceived of as the stuff occupying this space, and elasticity and rigidity could be ascribed to it.

If we turn to the experimental findings to which even the most abstruse hypothesis must appeal, if appeal is by any device possible, we find that the test takes place within what I have called the manipulatory area. We are here dealing with pointer readings that reflect changes lying at a distance from the changes in the apparatus. Within this manipulatory area visual perspectives disappear, and we can reach a high degree of accuracy in measurement. Its spatial structure, as we have seen, is that of the rigid body, and so far as physical tests can go it is that of Euclidean geometry. What is of peculiar importance is that it is within this field that we find, directly or indirectly, our common objects. For example, the penny with which epistemologists have been so much occupied is the same penny for different observers at different angles and at different distances in so far as these different visual pennies are recognized as appearances of one and the same penny which any of the observers, under the control of his visual experience, could touch and handle. As a result of a common method of manipulation, measurement and location, the manipulatory areas of the different observers thus become identical. It is important to recognize that while each individual will receive from the penny an experience of pressure, in a sense peculiar to himself, the method of identifying the penny that all will experience is not peculiar to himself. It is a logical procedure whose entities and relations exist only in so far as they constitute a universal factor in the experience of the individual. The individual, that is, does not first make his own measurements and reach his own identifications, and then compare these with those of others in order to reach a common object; his method of determination is rather in terms of a language that with its various symbols comes into existence only through the fact that the individual assumes the attitude common to all those involved in the common undertaking. This common penny attains the reality of experimental findings, however, only if it comes back directly or indirectly to a measurable something in the manipulatory area. At the basis of the process of measurement, of course, there lies the fundamental mechanism of perception, in which distance experiences lead to contact experiences that control the environment in the interest of the organism. The contact experiences are the reality of the distance experiences. The physical object, however, constitutes a break in the primitive biological process that finds its completion in the consummation which the biological needs of the organism call for. It is the hand under the control of the eye that is responsible for the manipulatory area. The handled object comes betwixt and between the vision of food and its eating. If the biological process, under the distance stimulation, goes through to consummation without interruption, no physical object arises in experience. In a biological sense the manipulated or physical object is thus a mediate reality. In its abstraction from consummation it is first of all an implement, and then the physical thing of a later science.

When the Michelson-Morley experiment and the difficulties brought to light by the lack of invariance in the Maxwell equations of electro-magnetism had ejected ether as a physical thing, the ether of "stuff," or, to use Whitehead's term, the event, was substituted for it, and time entered as a dimension of the physical thing. We have already seen that in the perceptual world space and time are inevitably separated. Motion involves a something that moves which is irrelevant to the temporal process. An event always happens to something. A striking result of recent changes in physical science, and of the new theories to which these changes have given rise, is that the event has taken the place of the physical thing. In the perceptual world and in the world of masses in motion events happen to things. Over against change there are unchanged things which are the conditions of change. That is, in the perceptual world space and time are necessarily separate. Space-time cannot be the form of perceptual experience. We can shift from one perspective to another, and realize that what from one standpoint is rest, from another is motion; but in each perspective there are permanent things, irrelevant to time, that give meaning to the changes that go on within time. If perspectives can be reduced to diverse appearances of things that have remained the same during all changes, relativity will not bite into the nature of the things; but if the nature of things is found in process, in a system of changes, the different values which this process takes on from the various standpoints of different but related observers must affect the natures of the things themselves. Yet we cannot really reduce things to processes, for it is not possible that processes should go on that are not processes of things, and measurements can only be made in a situation within which something abides irrelevant to time.

While the event is taking place we watch it or listen to it or feel it; but if we can complete the behavior it initiates, we isolate the thing to which the event is happening. But from the standpoint of relativity no physical object can be isolated from what is happening to it. If it is at rest in one consentient set under the measurement of a scientist, it is moving in another set; and not only are its measurements in time and space shifting with the relative velocities of the sets, but its inner content of mass varies also. There is nothing that can be laid hold of except the transformations of these measurements from one set to another and the coincidences of events in an absolute space. Now what this amounts to is that we have no sooner got hold of the thing in a permanent space within which we can measure it and determine its inner mass-content than we must put ourselves at a distance from it in another space and determine its changes due to the relative velocities of these two spaces and their consentient sets.

We have thus reversed the fundamental order of our behavior and have made the "what a thing is" a distance experience instead of a contact experience. The reason for this shifting is evident. The object in the manipulatory area belongs to the perspective of the individual, and, in so far as this manipulatory area can be determined by measurements which are common to all members of the community to which he belongs, to the space and time of the consentient set of which his organism as a physical thing is a member. It is only by putting ourselves in the distant consentient set that we can realize that the distortions the objects of that set suffer are the same as those our set undergoes when seen from that standpoint. Since there is no absolute space to which these differing standpoints can be referred, as the perspectives of vision can be referred to a common manipulatory area, there can be no manipulatory area to which these perspectives or frames of reference may be referred. The measuring-rod and the clock that gives the local time belong to the manipulatory area, and the quantities they measure will vary from one set to another. There is no common measuring rod, and no common clock, that all can accept. The different observers can only make use of formulae of transformation by which measurements made in one set can be read into those of another. We are left therefore with a language of distance light-signals which can refer to no object common to the experience of all. It is true that by application of the formulae we can isolate a constant value for the interval between the coincidences of events in a Minkowski space-time, and that this constant value may be regarded as the common reality to which all the different measurements, made from the standpoints of various perspectives, ultimately refer. This space-time, however, abstracts from every character in the distance experience whose meaning lies in its reference to a common physical object. Only those characters in the distance experience are left that refer to a single form of calculation common to all the different perspectives. It is this abstraction that makes it possible to assimilate time to space as a fourth dimension. For this calculation what is a time-interval in one perspective is a space-interval in another. It would, however, be a mistake to assume that we have thus passed into a field of communication in which our symbols have lost all significance except that of reference to a common referent. In fact we are still in a visual world, with a finite value for the velocity of light; only the physical thing to which that visual experience refers is stated in terms of a calculation-value common to an indefinite number of diverse visual experiences.

A similar criticism may be made of the view that would regard energy as constituting the nature of the physical thing. For the perceptual world there must be a system of things, and energy is the measure of the changes brought about in this system when a force is brought to bear upon it from without. Experiments, and the mathematical formulation in which thermodynamics has clothed the results of these experiments, however, have justified the conclusion that such measurement reveals only the potential energy within the system. How widely we are justified in spreading the generalization of the conservation of energy has been made the subject of dispute, though, as Poincaré has pointed out, we can always assume potential energy to keep the doctrine intact. When, however, we make this energy the nature of the thing, we are as necessarily passing out of the perceptual world as when we substitute space-time for space and time.

Energy, like space-time, is a transformation value. We select a process in the manipulatory field—the amount of work done—as the measure of energy; but what is measured is not stated as a function of the mass of the body, on the contrary mass itself is stated in terms of energy. Thus, when we reduce physical things either to space-time or to energy, we are in either case utilizing a process of measurement in a perceptual, manipulatory area to give the nature of the physical thing, while the nature thus ascribed to the physical thing does not belong to the field of the measurement. In the one case instead of the thing we set up an event located in a space-time that lies outside of experience; in the other, we appeal, as in Ostwald's view, to a metaphysical field equally remote from experience.

Reduction of mass to electro-magnetism would provide us with a further illustration, for electro-magnetism and light have thus been brought back to the same process—viz., that which relates an organism to distant objects. If mass could be stated in electro-magnetic terms we should have substituted the distance-value of the object for its manipulatory value. That it should be so stated, however, presupposes that we are using the wave formulation and not the corpuscular formulation for electro-magnetism, and that we are not driven to introduce the corpuscular concept,—the photon, into the theory of light.

This brings us to Professor Bridgman's program of rigidly reducing all our physical concepts to the operations we make use of in measurement.[1] His proposal seems to amount to an undertaking to bring the object back to the manipulatory area, but not to interpret the physical thing as a volume of mass in motion, but rather to redefine the physical thing of the manipulatory area in terms of its uses in scientific measurement. The simple Newtonian doctrine interpreted the light and heat of the sun as evidence of molecules of massive elements in violent motions; but the elements have now become particles of electricity that can conceivably be defined entirely in electro-magnetic terms, and this means

[1] "The Logic of Modern Physics," especially chapter 1.

that we can define them only in terms of mathematical formulations whose constants are certain pointer-readings. The mathematical formulations fix as exactly as possible the conditions under which we can obtain these pointer readings. We are thus getting a picture, not of the movements of manipulatory things, which, within the realm of our observations, are the conditions of our distance experiences, but of ideal conditions of control of manipulatory situations in which these distance experiences can be reproduced. If we conceive the sun as made up of electrons and protons, we can present in an imagined manipulatory area the movements of these particles, with their distances from each other and their velocities. We can present the electron and the proton as pressing toward each other and as held apart by the centrifugal force of the incredible velocity with which the electron revolves about the proton. But if we go on to picture the electron and proton as crushed together in the center of the sun, thus setting free, in the form of radiation, the electro-magnetic energy, including that of mass, which is the "what it is" of these electrical particles, we have transformed the stuff or manipulatory content of the thing into distance experience. The indestructibility of Newtonian mass reflected our fundamental attitude that what we get hold of is the permanent reality of what we see, hear and otherwise sense at a distance. If this permanent reality disappears in radiation, and this comes to us, say, in heat and light, or in the form of cosmic rays, it is no longer a distance experience *of anything*. The same is true of fields of force. We may say that they are events but there are no things to which the events happen at the location where they are.

I am not voicing a hankering after the fleshpots of what Whitehead has called the materialism of the Newtonian period. That view was afflicted by the bifurcation that

Whitehead deplored, and harbored the whole nest of epistemological problems that Lovejoy has extensively spread before us.[2] I am only insisting that whatever view we may take of the momentous changes that science has brought in its wake since electro-magnetism began to dominate its research and doctrine, we cannot get away from the perceptual findings that all science accepts as its most fundamental criterion of reality. The appeal of science to its perceptual findings as its criterion evidently involves more than any mere confirmation of distance experience by contact experience; the appeal is rather to the perceptual occurrence of events predicted on the basis of an hypothesis, in order to confirm that hypothesis. The importance of the perceptually real thing of the manipulatory area appears when an object of this sort can be identified under observation and experiment in an exceptional instance; consider, for example, the radiation of black bodies where the reality of the object as a perceptual thing must be accepted, wholly in advance of any further interpretation of it that a later hypothesis may give. Here we reach a something that maintains itself as an object that can be felt as seen. It is further evident that the reliability of measurements—of pointer readings—must be assured within this same perceptual field. Even if we can neither spread out the space and time of this area into the Euclidean space of the Newtonian doctrine, nor subdivide its perceptual things into Newtonian mass-particles, we nevertheless in some fashion relate the assumed reality of a universe that goes way beyond the boundaries of our perceptual experience to the decisive reality of the scientist's findings.

Even if we reduce our physical concepts to operational processes, we must confess that our physical things belong

---

[2] "The Revolt Against Dualism," passim.

to the field of our control—the field of measurement of changes in our experience. The causal antecedents of these changes can no longer be stated in terms of physical things, in the sense that they are conceivable permanent contact-experiences referred to by distance-experiences; but our relevant measurements must still take place by means of physical things. The causal antecedent may, for example, be both physical and mental. It may be an event with adjectives supplied by ingression from a world of eternal objects or universals. Or the expression for it may be an elaborate mathematical apparatus for carrying out exact measurements within the field of experiment and observation, as in Bridgman's *Logic of the Physical Sciences*. Or again it may be a logical pattern corresponding to some structure in a metaphysical world beyond experience—an absolute world of space-time whose coincidences of events and the intervals between them cannot appear in our relative spaces and times. But in no case can the nature of these elements of the subatomic, electro-magnetic world take the place of the physical mass-particles of Newtonian doctrine which could be conceived of as subdivisions of the massive objects that come under our own hands.

The breakdown of the Newtonian mechanical system was reached when, with the development of the laws of thermodynamics and of the theory of electro-magnetism, that meaning of physical things which fits our perceptual experience could no longer be applied to the so-called material universe. We now find that exactly determined distance-experiences occur, which answer to something going on—something, however, that cannot be stated in terms of changes among manipulatory things. In fact, we now postulate in our physical hypotheses, as the inner nature of the things referred to by the earlier distance experiences, other distance experiences, such as energies, or radiations. In the account given of the pressure of gases, on the other hand, we present to ourselves a picture of mass-particles bombarding each other and the walls of the container. Here the ultimate elements are physical things conceived in perceptual terms. But when we speak of the content of the electrons and protons as an energy which may take the form of radiation, we are describing them in terms of another distance experience—one which, moreover, can refer to no conceivable contact-experience. We cannot however simply brush to one side the whole of perceptual experience with the claim that we are dealing rather with the conceptual objects of science, for both our problems and our observations and experiments are stated in perceptual experience.

There are two sides to the question. I think we must admit that the distance-experience does and must imply that what is going on *there* would be responsible for contact-experiences if the organism could be at the place where the process responsible for the distance experience is going on, and were provided with the appropriate sensitivity. The other side of the question is, why do we state the nature of the object not in these terms but in terms of distance-experience? I assume that the reason for this is that the scientist is seeking for what is permanent, that he finds this in the uniformities of the processes, that it is in terms of these uniformities that he defines his objects, and that this therefore is what he means when he speaks of conceptual objects. The scientist seems thus to have transcended the perceptual field. He seems to be dealing no longer either with distance—or with contact-experience, but rather with an organized system of changes which may in perceptual experience reflect themselves in either of these categories, but which is really entirely independent of such experience. The door thus is thrown open to the representative theory of perception. The perceptual content of the object comes to be defined in terms of sense-data, which are correlated with scientific objects, but have their proper locus in a consciousness, or else lie somewhere between the mind and nature.

There are two reasons why the scientist does not make use of this realm of consciousness, either in terms of consciousness or in terms of sense data. The first is that the world which is out there in his observations and experiments is the world of reality. No satisfactory line can be drawn that will leave what is real for him on one side and sense-data on the other. This fact becomes particularly evident when we consider what we term the *meanings* of things. These are inextricably interwoven with what must be termed consciousness; yet these meanings are the very nature of the scientific objects. The other reason is that so-called consciousness has now been brought within the range of biologic science. Mind can no longer be put outside of nature.

As long as the scientist could be at home in a world of Newtonian mechanics, before the atom disintegrated into particles of electricity, he could look with Du Bois-Reymond's telescopic eye through the masses of things down to ultimate particles whose motions followed relatively simple laws. The connection of scientific with perceptual objects was close enough to make him feel that his observations and experiments were in the same world with the objects of his science. It is true that the so-called sensory qualities, whether secondary or primary, could not be the actual characters of the object; but the agreement between the Euclidean space of science and that of perception was adequate, and the correlation of weight with mass was so complete that the imaginary subdivision of the matter of sense-perception still paralleled the analyses of physics. The scientist was compelled, of course, so far as he considered the matter, to locate all secondary qualities in consciousness, since the mechanical universe consisted simply of mass-particles in motion, and of ether waves. In the physical world it was types of motion that corresponded to color, sound, taste, odor and temperature. If the scientist had been consistent he would have had to relegate to consciousness the resistances of things as well; but as a matter of fact nothing interfered with his building up mechanical models of mass-particles in his perceptual imagination of what was going on in nature. Lord Kelvin is an excellent example of the scientist of the period that had come to terms with thermo-dynamics and electro-magnetism, yet still sought to preserve in the vortices and stresses of the ether a mechanical picture of the anatomy of the universe within which the perceptual imagination could be at home. Millikan's oil-drops, Rutherford's photographs of the bombardment of atoms by alpha-particles, and the models of the Bohr atom, seemed to connect the galaxies of the sub-microscopical world with those of stellar space. As long as pushing and resistant things with calculable velocities could be located in space, scientific imagination did not leave the world of perception.

It is relativity that changed all this. In the geometry of a Minkowski space-time perceptual motion disappears. The ether has vanished, and events take the place of physical things. Time is assimilated to space, and the mind with its own spatial frame of reference adventures into this space-time whose curvature corresponds to the gravitational constant. The result is to carry the whole world of perception and perceptual imagination into perspectives that exhibit only a logical correlation between patterns affected with transformation formulae and events in a four dimensional time-space and intervals between them. By definition both events and intervals here lie outside of any experience. We reach them by way of the reference in the knowledge process to something beyond itself, and by a theory of probability. In our mathematical formulations of scientific experience we have come upon a cipher that seems to refer to inexperiencable entities and their mutual relations; and this hypostasized structure of logical entities satisfies our desire for an absolute reality to which our confessedly relative experience shall refer.

Yet, however far the scientists' procedure may go it never reaches any situation except one in which a transformation, or a possible transformation, takes place. If we ask for what lies back of all transformations, we are asking for something outside of any experience, whether actual or imaginary. We do, for example, postulate stages of development of the universe which antedate any possible human experience, but in imagination these are spread before an inner eye, or at least before a mind. If we exclude the imagination, we have the abstractions of symbolic analysis, which are of the same logical character as the transformation formulae to which I have referred. If I say that this is a color, and hold this color in its universality before my mind, I am isolating that which enables me to reduce any other visual experience to the present experience in so far as this is occupied with visual as distinct from auditory or sensuous qualities of things. There is a common way of acting toward all qualities that exist for the eye, as there is another way of acting toward those that exist for the ear; and the isolation of this typical reaction enables me to "transform" my conduct toward red into that toward blue, in so far as I am able to react to color by one response and to sound by another.

What we designate as "mental" is this attitude of isolation of common features that call out identical responses provided that we have symbols by which we refer to them. To set up a world of essences or universals or eternal objects within which these entities subsist or exist is parallel to the procedure of setting up a Minkowski space-time or a four dimensional aggregate of events. Presumably objects in motion with reference to us have different values spatially, temporally and in terms of mass from those at rest; and if we are to measure them as we measure objects at rest about us we must isolate the common feature—viz., the relational character of space and time common to the two situations of rest and motion. The expression of this common feature in the transformation formulae that Larmor and Lorentz worked out in order to give invariance to the Maxwell equations carries with it most interesting implications, especially with reference to the constant velocity of light; but it does not change the fact that what is going on is measurement in one situation of something whose measurable characters are partly dependent upon the fact that it is in another situation as well. It does not carry with it the necessity of setting up a space-time realm. The postulation of such a realm rests upon the assumption that because the same object may be dealt with either as at rest or in motion, it must therefore be affected with the coördinate of time in the same fashion in each situation. This assumption consequently wipes out motion and substitutes for it geometrical determination in a four dimensional realm outside of any possible experience.

It all comes back to this; the separation of space and time is essential to the perceptual fact of motion. There must be a timeless space within which motion takes place. But timeless spaces differ according as the individual or "percipient event" is in motion or at rest. If, as in the example of the railway train, we transfer ourselves from the space of the compartment within the train to that of the landscape, then the space of the compartment within the train is in motion, and that space, if measured, will be measured in units differing from those of the space of the landscape. The same is true of the times. Given the relational character of space and time, their structural characters differ according to what may be called the temporal perspective of the individual. And, as Whitehead insists, these differences belong to nature. They are not subjective. But the scientist is satisfied with the transformation from one situation to another. Whether he accepts a geometry of space-time or not, his operation is occupied only with the transformation and does not require the assumption of a transcendent space-time. The physicist's aim is an invariant set of equations that will formulate the conditions under which we may control our physical conduct. In order to reach an invariance for the Maxwell equations, and to interpret the Michelson-Morley experiment, it became necessary to work out transformations from one temporal perspective to another. The possibility of successful formulae of transformation involves numerical statements identical for all different perspectives. These can be expressed in terms of intersections of events, and intervals between them, in an absolute space-time; but such a formulation is not made use of in the physicist's transformations. In every instance the physicist is in a perceptual world, transforming, so far as may be necessary, one perceptual perspective into another. Nor is the situation changed when we pass from the special to the general principle of relativity. In the application of the special theory the coördinates have immediate physical significance, denoting measures expressed in terms of standard measuring-rods and clocks, while in the general theory the numbers refer to a continuum lying, as we have seen, outside of any possible experience. The constants remain therefore mere numbers in terms of which natural laws can be so expressed that they hold in any frame of reference, that a transformation of axes of coördinate systems may be substituted for a field of gravitational force, and, in general, that the metrical properties of space are wholly determined by the masses of bodies. Einstein's genius has on the basis of these principles elaborated a physical theory which not only carries through to logical completeness the relativity of space and time, but also gives a more perfect and accurate formulation of physical processes—one, moreover, that has stood the test of observation and experiment at those points at which it could be brought to the test. In the special theory we are formulating measurable values—in terms of different systems of coördinates—for one perceptual perspective in terms of another perceptual perspective, i.e., we are dealing with local times and local measuring rods. The numbers have physical significance. In the general theory we obtain equations that are covariant, i.e., we do not transform from one set of coördinates to another, but obtain expressions that hold for all possible sets of coördinates. The numbers evidently cannot express the measures of time and space in any one coördinate system, as distinct from another. They arise out of the possibility of transformation from any possible set to any other possible set. They are reached by the use of a Riemannian geometry of a four-dimensional manifold, and tensor mathematics. These provide the mathematical apparatus for the measurement of the intervals in a continuum however it may be deformed—a continuum, in this case, of space-time, and determine the form which equations that express natural laws must have if they are to hold for every set of coördinates.

It is as if we should take the formula by which we transform the value of the dollar in 1913 into that of 1930, and into that of any other possible date in human history, and should pass over from the constants of food, clothing and the like and what they will exchange for, to a generalized economic field in which the distances between the exchange-

constant of gravitation will prove to be such as not to resolve itself into curvatures of space-time. I recur to the statement I made earlier, that the reference of general relativity as well as that of special relativity is to the field of experience within which scientific problems, observations and experiments lie.

IV

The Objective Reality of Perspectives[1]

The grandiose undertaking of Absolute Idealism to bring the whole of reality within experience failed. It failed because it left the perspective of the finite ego hopelessly infected with subjectivity and consequently unreal. From its point of view the theoretical and practical life of the individual had no part in the creative advance of nature. It failed also because scientific method, with its achievements of discovery and invention, could find no adequate statement in its dialectic. It recognized the two dominant forces of modern life, the creative individual and creative science only to abrogate them as falsifications of the experience of the absolute ego. The task remained unfulfilled, the task of restoring to nature the characters and qualities which a metaphysics of mind and a science of matter and motion had concurred in relegating to consciousness, and of finding such a place for mind in nature that nature could appear in experience. A constructive restatement of the problem was presented by a physiological and experimental psychology that fastened mind inextricably in an organic nature which both science and philosophy recognized. The dividend which philosophy declared upon this restatement is indicated in William James's reasoned query "Does Consciousness exist?" The metaphysical assault upon the dualism of mind and nature, that has been becoming every day more intolerable, has been made in regular formation by Bergson's evolutionary philosophy, by neo-idealism, by

[1] Reprinted by permission from the Proceedings of the Sixth International Congress of Philosophy.

sonian edition of Spinoza's underlying substance that individualizes itself in the structure of the events, nor his Platonic heaven of eternal objects where lie the hierarchies of patterns, that are there envisaged as possibilities and have ingression into events, but rather his Leibnizian filiation, as it appears in his conception of the perspective as the mirroring in the event of all other events. Leibniz made a psychological process central in his philosophy of nature. The contents of his monads were psychical states, perceptions, and *petites perceptions,* which were inevitably representative of the rest of the reality of the universe of which they were but partially developed expressions. The represented content of all monads was identical, in so far as it was clear and distinct, so that the organization of these perspectives was a harmony preëstablished in an identity of rational content. Professor Whitehead's principle of organization of perspectives is not the representation of an identical content, but the intersection by different time systems of the same body of events. It is, of course, the abandonment of simple location as the principle of physical existence, i.e., that the existence of a physical object is found in its occupancy of a certain volume of absolute space in an instant of absolute time; and the taking of time seriously, i.e., the recognition that there are an indefinite number of possible simultaneities of any event with other events, and consequently an indefinite number of possible temporal orders of the same events, that make it possible to conceive of the same body of events as organized into an indefinite number of different perspectives.

Without undertaking to discuss Professor Whitehead's doctrine of the prehension into the unity of the event of the aspects of other events, which I am unable to work out satisfactorily, from the summary statements I have found in his writings, I wish to consider the conception of a body of events as the organization of different perspectives of these events, from the standpoint of the field of social science, and that of behavioristic psychology.

In the first place, this seems to be exactly the subject matter of any social science. The human experience with which social science occupies itself is primarily that of individuals. It is only so far as the happenings, the environmental conditions, the values, their uniformities and laws enter into the experience of individuals as individuals that they become the subject of consideration by these sciences. Environmental conditions, for example, exist only in so far as they affect actual individuals, and only as they affect these individuals. The laws of these happenings are but the statistical uniformities of the happenings to and in the experiences of A, B, C, and D. Furthermore the import of these happenings and these values must be found in the experiences of these individuals if they are to exist for these sciences at all.

In the second place, it is only in so far as the individual acts not only in his own perspective but also in the perspective of others, especially in the common perspective of a group, that a society arises and its affairs become the object of scientific inquiry. The limitation of social organization is found in the inability of individuals to place themselves in the perspectives of others, to take their points of view. I do not wish to belabor the point, which is commonplace enough, but to suggest that we find here an actual organization of perspectives, and that the principle of it is fairly evident. This principle is that the individual enters into the perspectives of others, in so far as he is able to take their attitudes, or occupy their points of view.

But while the principle is a commonplace for social conduct, its implications are very serious if one accepts the objectivity of perspectives, and recognizes that these perspectives are made up of other selves with minds; that here is no nature that can be closed to mind. The social perspective exists in the experience of the individual in so far as it is intelligible, and it is its intelligibility that is the condition of the individual entering into the perspectives of others, especially of the group. In the field of any social science the objective data are those experiences of the individuals in which they take the attitude of the community, i.e., in which they enter into the perspectives of the other members of the community. Of course the social scientist may generalize from the standpoint of his universe of discourse what remains hopelessly subjective in the experiences of another community, as the psychologist can interpret what for the individual is an unintelligible feeling. I am speaking not from the standpoint of the epistemologist, nor that of the metaphysician. I am asking simply what is objective for the social scientist, what is the subject matter of his science, and I wish to point out that the critical scientist is only replacing the narrower social perspectives of other communities by that of a more highly organized and hence more universal community.

It is instructive to note that never has the character of that common perspective changed more rapidly than since we have gained further control over the technique by which the individual perspective becomes the perspective of the most universal community, that of thinking men, that is, the technique of the experimental method. We are deluded, by the ease with which we can, by what may be fairly called transformation formulae, translate the experience of other communities into that of our own, into giving finality to the perspective of our own thought; but a glance at the bewildering rapidity with which different histories, i.e., different pasts have succeeded each other, and new physical universes have arisen, is sufficient to assure us that no generation has been so uncertain as to what will be the common perspective of the next. We have never been so uncertain as to what are the values which economics undertakes to define, what are the political rights and obligations of citizens, what are the community values of friendship, of passion, of parenthood, of amusement, of beauty, of social solidarity in its unnumbered forms, or of those values which have been gathered under the relations of man to the highest community or to God. On the other hand there has never been a time at which men could determine so readily the conditions under which values, whatever they are, can be secured. In terms of common conditions, by transformation formulae, we can pass from one value field to another, and thus come nearer finding out which is more valuable, or rather how to conserve each. The common perspective is comprehensibility, and comprehensibility is the statement in terms of common social conditions.

It is the relation of the individual perspective to the common perspective that is of importance. To the biologist there is a common environment of an ant-hill or of a beehive, which is rendered possible by the intricate social relationships of the ants and the bees. It is entirely improbable that this perspective exists in the perspectives of individual ants or bees, for there is no evidence of communication. Communication is a social process whose natural history shows that it arises out of coöperative activities, such as those involved in sex, parenthood, fighting, herding, and the like, in which some phase of the act of one form, which may be called a gesture, acts as a stimulus to others to carry on their parts of the social act. It does not become communication in the full sense, i.e., the stimulus does not become a significant symbol, until the gesture tends to arouse the same response in the individual who makes it that it arouses in the others. The history of the growth of language shows that in its earlier stages the vocal gesture addressed to another awakens in the individual who makes the gesture not simply the tendency to the response which it calls forth in the other, such as the seizing of a weapon or the avoiding of a danger, but primarily the social rôle which the other plays in the coöperative act. This is indicated in the early play period in the development of the child, and in the richness in social implication of language structures in the speech of primitive peoples.

In the process of communication the individual is an other before he is a self. It is in addressing himself in the rôle of an other that his self arises in experience. The growth of the organized game out of simple play in the experience of the child, and of organized group activities in human society, placed the individual then in a variety of rôles, in so far as these were parts of the social act, and the very organization of these in the whole act gave them a common character in indicating what he had to do. He is able then to become a generalized other in addressing himself in the attitude of the group or the community. In this situation he has become a definite self over against the social whole to which he belongs. This is the common perspective. It exists in the organisms of all the members of the community, because the physiological differentiation of human forms belongs largely to the consummatory phase of the act.

The overt phase within which social organization takes place is occupied with things, physical things or implements. In the societies of the invertebrates, which have indeed a complexity comparable with human societies, the organization is largely dependent upon physiological differentiation. In such a society, evidently, there is no phase of the act of the individual in which he can find himself taking the attitude of the other. Physiological differentiation, apart from the direct relations of sex and parenthood, plays no part in the organization of human society. The mechanism of human society is that of bodily selves who assist or hinder each other in their coöperative acts by the manipulation of physical things. In the earliest forms of society these physical things are treated as selves, i.e., those social responses, which we can all detect in ourselves to inanimate things which aid or hinder us, are dominant among primitive peoples in the social organization that depends on the use of physical means. The primitive man keeps *en rapport* with implements and weapons by conversation in the form of magic rites and ceremonies. On the other hand the bodily selves of members of the social group are as clearly implemental as the implements are social. Social beings are things as definitely as physical things are social.

The key to the genetic development of human intelligence is found in the recognition of these two aspects. It arises in those early stages of communication in which the organism arouses in itself the attitude of the other and so addresses itself and thus becomes an object to itself, becomes in other words a self, while the same sort of content in the act constitutes the other that constitutes the self. Out of this process thought arises, i.e., conversation with one's self, in the rôle of the specific other and then in the rôle of the generalized other, in the fashion I indicated above. It is important to recognize that the self does not project itself into the other. The others and the self arise in the social act together. The content of the act may be said to lie within the organism but it is projected into the other only in the sense in which it is projected into the self, a fact upon which the whole of psycho-analysis rests. We pinch ourselves to be sure that we are awake as we grasp an object to be sure that it is there. The other phase of human intelligence is that it is occupied with physical things. Physical things are perceptual things. They also arise within the act. This is initiated by a distant stimulus and leads through approximation or withdrawal to contact or the avoidance of contact. The outcome of the act is in consummation, e.g., as in eating, but in the behavior of the human animal a mediate stage of manipulation intervenes. The hand fashions the physical or perceptual thing. The perceptual thing is fully there in the manipulatory area, where it is both seen and felt, where is found both the promise of the contact and its fulfilment, for it is characteristic of the distant stimulation and the act that it initiates that there are already aroused the attitudes of manipulation,—what I will call terminal attitudes of the perceptual act, that readiness to grasp, to come into effective contact, which in some sense control the approach to the distant stimulation. It is in the operation with these perceptual or physical things which lie within the physiological act short of consummation that the peculiar human intelligence is found. Man is an implemental animal. It is mediate to consummation. The hand carries the food to the mouth, or the child to the breast, but in the social act this mediation becomes indefinitely complicated, and the task arises of stating the consummation, or the end, in terms of means. There are two conditions for this: one is the inhibition, which takes place when conflicting ways of completing the act check the expression of any one way, and the other is the operation of the social mechanism, which I have described, by which the individual can indicate to others and to himself the perceptual things that can be seized and manipulated and combined. It is within this field of implemental things picked out by the significant symbols of gesture, not in that of physiological differentiation, that the complexities of human society have developed. And, to recur to my former statement, in this field selves are implemental physical things just as among primitive peoples physical things are selves.

My suggestion was that we find in society and social experience, interpreted in terms of a behavioristic psychology, an instance of that organization of perspectives, which is for me at least the most obscure phase of Professor Whitehead's philosophy. In his objective statement of relativity the existence of motion in the passage of events depends not upon what is taking place in an absolute space and time, but upon the relation of a consentient set to a percipient event. Such a relation stratifies nature. These stratifications are not only there in nature but they are the only forms of nature that are there. This dependence of nature upon the percipient event is not a reflection of nature into consciousness. Permanent spaces and times, which are successions of these strata, rest and motion, are there, but they are there only in their relationship to percipient events or organisms. We can then go further and say that the sensuous qualities of nature are there in nature, but there in their relationship to animal organisms. We can advance to the other values which have been regarded as dependent upon appetence, appreciation, and affection, and thus restore to nature all that a dualistic doctrine has relegated to consciousness, since the spatio-temporal structure of the world and the motion with which exact physical science is occupied is found to exist in nature only in its relationship to percipient events or organisms.

But rest and motion no more imply each other than do objectivity and subjectivity. There are perspectives which cease to be objective, such as the Ptolemaic order, since it does not select those consentient sets with the proper dynamical axes, and there are those behind the mirror and those of an alcoholic brain. What has happened in all of these instances, from the most universal to the most particular, is that the rejected perspective fails to agree with that common perspective which the individual finds himself occupying as a member of the community of minds, which is constitutive of his self. This is not a case of the surrender to a vote of the majority, but the development of another self through its intercourse with others and hence with himself.

What I am suggesting is that this process, in which a perspective ceases to be objective, becomes if you like subjective, and in which new common minds and new common perspectives arise, is an instance of the organization of perspectives in nature, of the creative advance of nature. This amounts to the affirmation that mind as it appears in the mechanism of social conduct is the organization of perspectives in nature and at least a phase of the creative advance of nature. Nature in its relationship to the organism, and including the organism, is a perspective that is there. A state of mind of the organism is the establishment of simultaneity between the organism and a group of events, through the arrest of action under inhibition as above described. This arrest of action means the tendencies within the organism to act in conflicting ways in the completion of the whole act. The attitude of the organism calls out or tends to call out responses in other organisms, which responses, in the case of human gesture, the organism calls out in itself, and thus excites itself to respond to these responses. It is the identification of these responses with the distant stimuli that establishes simultaneity, that gives insides to these distant stimuli, and a self to the organism. Without such an establishment of simultaneity, these stimuli are spatio-temporally distant from the organism, and their reality lies in the future of passage. The establishment of simultaneity wrenches this future reality into a possible present, for all our presents beyond the manipulatory area are only possibilities, as respects their perceptual reality. We are acting toward the future realization of the act, as if it were present, because the organism is taking the rôle of the other. In the perceptual inanimate object the organic content that survives is the resistance that the organism both feels and exerts in the manipulatory area. The actual spatio-temporal structure of passing events with those characters which answer to the susceptibilities of the organism are there in nature, but they are temporally as well as spatially away from the organism. The reality awaits upon the success of the act. Present reality is a possibility. It is what would be if we were there instead of here. Through the social mechanism of significant symbols the organism places itself there as a possibility, which acquires increasing probability as it fits into the spatio-temporal structure and the demands of the whole complex act of which its conduct is a part. But the possibility is there in nature, for it is made up of actual structures of events and their contents, and the possible realizations of the acts in the form of adjustments and readjustments of the processes involved. When we view them as possibilities we call them mental or working hypotheses.

I submit that the only instance we have of prehension in experience is this holding together of future and past as possibilities—for all pasts are as essentially subject to revision as the futures, and are, therefore, only possibilities—and the common content which endures is that which is common to the organism and environment in the perspective. This in the organism is identified with the spatio-temporally distant stimuli as a possibly real present, past, and future. The unity lies in the act or process, the prehension is the exercise of this unity, when the process has been checked through conflicting tendencies, and the conditions and results of these tendencies are held as possibilities in a specious present.

Thus the social and psychological process is but an instance of what takes place in nature, if nature is an evolution, i.e., if it proceeds by reconstruction in the presence of conflicts, and if, therefore, possibilities of different reconstructions are present, reconstructing its pasts as well as its futures. It is the relativity of time, that is, an indefinite number of possible orders of events, that introduces possibility in nature. When there was but one recognized order of nature, possibility had no other place than in the mental constructions of the future or the incompletely known past. But the reality of a spatio-temporally distant situation lies ahead, and any present existence of it, beyond the manipulatory area, can be only a possibility. Certain characters are there, but what *things* they are can only be realized when the acts these distant stimulations arouse are completed. What they are now is represented by a set of possible spatio-temporal structures. That these future realizations appear as present possibilities is due to the arrest of the act of the organism, and its ability to indicate these possibilities.

That these possibilities have varying degrees of probability is due to the relation of the various inhibited tendencies in the organism to the whole act. The organization of this whole act the human social organism can indicate to others and to itself. It has the pattern which determines other selves and physical things, and the organism as a self and a thing, and the meanings which are indicated have the universality of the whole community to which the organism belongs. They constitute a universe of discourse. It is the fitting in of the particular tendencies into this larger pattern of the whole process that constitutes the probability of the present existence of the things which any one act implies. Its full reality is still dependent upon the accomplishment of the act, upon experimental evidence. It is then such a coincidence of the perspective of the individual organism with the pattern of the whole act in which it is so involved that the organism can act within it, that constitutes the objectivity of the perspective.

The pattern of the whole social act can lie in the individual organism because it is carried out through implemental things to which any organism can react, and because indications of these reactions to others and the organism itself can be made by significant symbols. The reconstruction of the pattern can take place in the organism, and does take place in the so-called conscious process of mind. The psychological process is an instance of the creative advance of nature.

In living forms lower than man the distant perspective may through sensitivity exist in the experience of the form and the grasping of this in the adjustments of conduct answer to the formation of the stratification of nature, but the reconstruction of the pattern within which the life of the organism lies does not fall within the experience of the organism. In inanimate organisms the maintenance of a temporal structure, i.e., of a process, still stratifies nature, and gives rise to spaces and times, but neither they nor the entities that occupy them enter as experiential facts into the processes of the organisms. The distinction of objectivity and subjectivity can only arise where the pattern of the larger process, within which lies the process of the individual organism, falls in some degree within the experience of the individual organism, i.e., it belongs only to the experience of the social organism.

V

The Genesis of the Self and Social Control[1]

It is evident that a statement of the life of each individual in terms of the results of an analysis of that which is immediately experienced would offer a common plane of events, in which the experience of each would differ from the experiences of others only in their extent, and the completeness or incompleteness of their connections. These differences disappear in the generalized formulations of the social sciences. The experiences of the same individuals, in so far as each faces a world in which objects are plans of action, would implicate in each a different succession of events. In the simplest illustration, two persons approach a passing automobile. To one it is a moving object that he will pass before it reaches the portion of the street that is the meeting-place of their two paths. The other sees an object that will pass this meeting-point before he reaches it. Each slices the world from the standpoint of a different time system. Objects which in a thousand ways are identical for the two individuals, are yet fundamentally different through their location in one spatio-temporal plane, involving a certain succession of events, or in another. Eliminate the temporal dimension, and bring all events back to an instant that is timeless, and the individuality of these objects which belongs to them in behavior is lost, except in so far as they can represent the results of past conduct. But taking time seriously, we realize that the seemingly timeless character of our spatial world and its permanent objects

[1] Reprinted in part from "The International Journal of Ethics," Vol. 35, No. 3, April 1925.

is due to the consentient set which each one of us selects. We abstract time from this space for the purposes of our conduct. Certain objects cease to be events, cease to pass as they are in reality passing and in their permanence become the conditions of our action, and events take place with reference to them. Because a whole community selects the same consentient set does not make the selection less the attitude of each one of them. The life-process takes place in individual organisms, so that the psychology which studies that process in its creative determining function becomes a science of the objective world.

Looked at from the standpoint of an evolutionary history, not only have new forms with their different spatio-temporal environments and their objects arisen, but new characters have arisen answering to the sensitivities and capacities for response. In the terms of Alexander, they have become differently qualitied. It is as impossible to transfer these characters of the habitats to the consciousness of the forms as it is to transfer the spatio-temporal structure of the things to such a so-called consciousness. If we introduce a fictitious instantaneousness into a passing universe, things fall to pieces. Things that are spatio-temporally distant from us can be brought into this instant only in terms of our immediate contact experience. They are what they would be if we were there and had our hands upon them. They take on the character of tangible matter. This is the price of their being located at the moment of our bodies' existence. But this instantaneous view has the great advantage of giving to us a picture of what the contact experience will be when we reach the distant object, and of determining conditions under which the distance characters arise. If the world existed at an instant in experience, we should be forced to find some realm such as consciousness into which to transport the distance or so-called secondary qualities of things. If consciousness in evolutionary history, then, has an unambiguous significance, it refers to that stage in the development of life in which the conduct of the individual marks out and defines the future field and objects which make up its environment, and in which emerge characters in the objects and sensitivities in the individuals that answer to each other. There is a relativity of the living individual and its environment, both as to form and content.

What I wish to trace is the fashion in which self and the mind has arisen within this conduct.

It is the implication of this undertaking that only selves have minds, that is, that cognition only belongs to selves, even in the simplest expression of awareness. This, of course, does not imply that below the stage of self-consciousness sense characters and sensitivity do not exist. This obtains in our own immediate experience in so far as we are not self-conscious. It is further implied that this development has taken place only in a social group, for selves exist only in relation to other selves, as the organism as a physical object exists only in its relation to other physical objects. There have been two fields within which social groups have arisen which have determined their environment together with that of their members, and the individuality of its members. These lie in the realm of the invertebrates and in that of the vertebrates. Among the Hymenoptera and termites there are societies whose interests determine for the individuals their stimuli and habitats, and so differentiate the individuals themselves, mainly through the sexual and alimentary processes, that the individual is what he is because of his membership within those societies. In the complex life of the group, the acts of the individuals are completed only through the acts of other individuals, but the mediation of this complex conduct is found in the physiological differentiation of the different members of the society. As Bergson has remarked of the instincts, the implements by which a complex act is carried out are found in the differentiated structure of the form. There is no convincing evidence that an ant or a bee is obliged to anticipate the act of another ant or bee, by tending to respond in the fashion of the other, in order that it may integrate its activity into the common act. And by the same mark there is no evidence of the existence of any language in their societies. Nor do we need to go to the invertebrates to discover this type of social conduct. If one picks up a little child who has fallen, he adapts his arms and attitude to the attitude of the child, and the child adapts himself to the attitude of the other; or in boxing or fencing one responds to stimulus of the other, by acquired physiological adjustment.

Among the vertebrates, apart from the differentiation of the sexes and the nurture and care of infant forms, there is little or no inherited physiological differentiation to mediate the complexities of social conduct. If we are to coöperate successfully with others, we must in some manner get their ongoing acts into ourselves to make the common act come off. As I have just indicated, there is a small range of social activity in which this is not necessary. The suckling of an infant form, or a dog fight, if this may be called a social activity, does not call for more than inherited physiological adjustment. Perhaps the so-called herding instinct should be added, but it hardly comes to more than the tendency of the herd to stick together in their various activities. The wooing and mating of forms, the care of the infant form, the bunching of animals in migrations, and fighting, about exhaust vertebrate social conduct, and beyond these seasonal processes vertebrate societies hardly exist till we reach man. They exhaust the possibilities in vertebrate structure of the mediation of social conduct, for the vertebrate organism has shown no such astonishing plasticity in physiological differentiation as that which we can trace among the insects, from isolated forms to members of the societies of the termites, the ants, and the bees.

A social act may be defined as one in which the occasion or stimulus which sets free an impulse is found in the character or conduct of a living form that belongs to the proper environment of the living form whose impulse it is. I wish, however, to restrict the social act to the class of acts which involve the coöperation of more than one individual, and whose object as defined by the act, in the sense of Bergson, is a social object. I mean by a social object one that answers to all the parts of the complex act, though these parts are found in the conduct of different individuals. The objective of the act is then found in the life-process of the group, not in those of the separate individuals alone. The full social object would not exist in the environments of the separate individuals of the societies of the Hymanoptera and termites, nor in the restricted societies of the vertebrates whose basis is found alone in physiological adjustment. A cow that licks the skin of a calf stuffed with hay, until the skin is worn away, and then eats the hay, or a woman who expends her parental impulse upon a poodle, cannot be said to have the full social object involved in the entire act in their environments. It would be necessary to piece together the environments of the different individuals or superimpose them upon each other to reach the environment and objects of the societies in question.

Where forms such as those of the Hymenoptera and the termites exhibit great plasticity in development, social acts based on physiological adjustment, and corresponding societies, have reached astonishing complexity. But when the limit of that plasticity is reached, the limit of the social act and the society is reached also. Where, as among the vertebrates, that physiological adjustment which mediates a social act is limited and fixed, the societies of this type are correspondingly insignificant. But another type of social act, and its corresponding society and object, has been at least suggested by the description of the social act based upon physiological adjustment. Such an act would be one in which the different parts of the act which belong to different individuals should appear in the act of each individual. This cannot mean, however, that the single individual could carry out the entire act, for then, even if it were possible, it would cease to be a social act, nor could the stimulus which calls out his own part of the complex act be that which calls out the other parts of the act in so far as they appear in his conduct. If the social object is to appear in his experience, it must be that the stimuli which set free the responses of the others involved in the act should be present in his experience, not as stimuli to his response, but as stimuli for the responses of others; and this implies that the social situation which arises after the completion of one phase of the act, which serves as the stimulus for the next participant in the complex procedure, shall in some sense be in the experience of the first actor, tending to call out, not his own response, but that of the succeeding actor. Let us make the impossible assumption that the wasp, in stinging a spider which it stores with its egg, finds in the spider a social object in the sense which I have specified. The spider would have to exist in the experience of the wasp as live but quiescent food for the larva when it emerges from the egg. In order that the paralyzed spider should so appear to the wasp, the wasp would need to be subject to the same stimulus as that which sets free the response of the larva; in other words, the wasp would need to be able to respond in some degree as the

in exchange, and appear as essential features of the individual's action.

The individual in such an act is a self. If the cortex has become an organ of social conduct, and has made possible the appearance of social objects, it is because the individual has become a self, that is, an individual who organizes his own response by the tendencies on the part of others to respond to his act. He can do this because the mechanism of the vertebrate brain enables the individual to take these different attitudes in the formation of the act. But selves have appeared late in vertebrate evolution. The structure of the central nervous system is too minute to enable us to show the corresponding structural changes in the paths of the brain. It is only in the behavior of the human animal that we can trace this evolution. It has been customary to mark this stage in development by endowing man with a mind, or at least with a certain sort of mind. As long as consciousness is regarded as a sort of spiritual stuff out of which are fashioned sensations and affections and images and ideas or significances, a mind as a locus of these entities is an almost necessary assumption, but when these contents have been returned to things, the necessity of quarters for this furniture has disappeared also.

It lies beyond the bounds of this paper to follow out the implications of this shift for logic and epistemology, but there is one phase of all so-called mental processes which is central to this discussion, and that is self-consciousness. If the suggestions which I have made above should prove tenable, the self that is central to all so-called mental experience has appeared only in the social conduct of human vertebrates. It is just because the individual finds himself taking the attitudes of the others who are involved in his conduct that he becomes an object for himself. It is only by taking the rôles of others that we have been able to come back to ourselves. We have seen above that the social object can exist for the individual only if the various parts of the whole social act carried out by other members of the society are in some fashion present in the conduct of the individual. It is further true that the self can exist for the individual only if he assumes the rôles of the others. The presence in the conduct of the individual of the tendencies to act as others act may be, then, responsible for the appearance in the experience of the individual of a social object, i.e., an object answering to complex reactions of a number of individuals, and also for the appearance of the self. Indeed, these two appearances are correlative. Property can appear as an object only in so far as the individual stimulates himself to buy by a prospective offer to sell. Buying and selling are involved in each other. Something that can be exchanged can exist in the experience of the individual only in so far as he has in his own make-up the tendency to sell when he has also the tendency to buy. And he becomes a self in his experience only in so far as one attitude on his own part calls out the corresponding attitude in the social undertaking.

This is just what we imply in "self-consciousness." We appear as selves in our conduct in so far as we ourselves take the attitude that others take toward us, in these correlative activities. Perhaps as good an illustration of this as can be found is in a "right." Over against the protection of our lives or property, we assume the attitude of assent of all members in the community. We take the rôle of what may be called the "generalized other." And in doing this we appear as social objects, as selves. It is interesting to note that in the development of the individual child, there are two stages which present the two essential steps in attaining self-consciousness. The first stage is that of play, and the second that of the game, where these two are distinguished from each other. In play in this sense, the child is continually acting as a parent, a teacher, a preacher, a grocery man, a policeman, a pirate, or an Indian. It is the period of childish existence which Wordsworth has described as that of "endless imitation." It is the period of Froebel's kindergarten plays. In it, as Froebel recognized, the child is acquiring the rôles of those who belong to his society. This takes place because the child is continually exciting in himself the responses to his own social acts. In his infant dependence upon the responses of others to his own social stimuli, he is peculiarly sensitive to this relation. Having in his own nature the beginning of the parental response, he calls it out by his own appeals. The doll is the universal type of this, but before he plays with a doll, he responds in tone of voice and in attitude as his parents respond to his own cries and chortles. This has been denominated imitation, but the psychologist now recognizes that one imitates only in so far as the so-called imitated act can be called out in the individual by his appropriate stimulation. That is, one calls or tends to call out in himself the same response that he calls out in the other.

The play antedates the game. For in a game there is a regulated procedure, and rules. The child must not only take the rôle of the other, as he does in the play, but he must assume the various rôles of all the participants in the game, and govern his action accordingly. If he plays first base, it is as the one to whom the ball will be thrown from the field or from the catcher. Their organized reactions to him he has imbedded in his own playing of the different positions, and this organized reaction becomes what I have called the "generalized other" that accompanies and controls his conduct. And it is this generalized other in his experience which provides him with a self. I can only refer to the bearing of this childish play attitude upon so-called sympathetic magic. Primitive men call out in their own activity some simulacrum of the response which they are seeking from the world about. They are children crying in the night.

The mechanism of this implies that the individual who is stimulating others to response is at the same time arousing in himself the tendencies to the same reactions. Now, that in a complex social act, which serves as the stimulus to another individual to his response is not as a rule fitted to call out the tendency to the same response in the individual himself. The hostile demeanor of one animal does not frighten the animal himself, presumably. Especially in the complex social reactions of the ants or termites or the bees, the part of the act of one form which does call out the appropriate reaction of another can hardly be conceived of as arousing a like reaction in the form in question, for here the complex social act is dependent upon physiological differentiation, such an unlikeness in structure exists that the same stimulus could not call out like responses. For such a mechanism as has been suggested, it is necessary to find first of all some stimulus in the social conduct of the members of an authentic group that can call out in the individual that is responsible for it, the same response that it calls out in the other; and in the second place, the individuals in the group must be of such like structure that the stimulus will have the same value for one form that it has for the other. Such a type of social stimulus is found in the vocal gesture in a human society. The term gesture I am using to refer to that part of the act or attitude of one individual engaged in a social act which serves as the stimulus to another individual to carry out his part of the whole act. Illustrations of gestures, so defined, may be found in the attitudes and movements of others to which we respond in passing them in a crowd, in the turning of the head toward the glance of another's eye, in the hostile attitude assumed over against a threatening gesture, in the thousand and one different attitudes which we assume toward different modulations of the human voice, or in the attitudes and suggestions of movements in boxers or fencers, to which responses are so nicely adjusted. It is to be noted that the attitudes to which I have referred are but stages in the act as they appear to others, and include expressions of countenance, positions of the body, changes in breathing rhythm, outward evidence of circulatory changes, and vocal sounds. In general these so-called gestures belong to the beginning of the overt act, for the adjustments of others to the social process are best made early in the act. Gestures are, then, the early stages in the overt social act to which other forms involved in the same act respond. Our interest is in finding gestures which can affect the individual that is responsible for them in the same manner as that in which they affect other individuals. The vocal gesture is at least one that assails our ears who make it in the same physiological fashion as that in which it affects others. We hear our own vocal gestures as others hear them. We may see or feel movements of our hands as others see or feel them, and these sights and feels have served in the place of the vocal gestures in the case of those who are congenitally deaf or deaf and blind. But it has been the vocal gesture that has preëminently provided the medium of social organization in human society. It belongs historically to the beginning of the act, for it arises out of the change in breathing rhythm that accompanies the preparation for sudden action, those actions to which other forms must be nicely adjusted.

If, then, a vocal gesture arouses in the individual who makes it a tendency to the same response that it arouses in another, and this beginning of an act of the other in himself enters into his experience, he will find himself tending to act toward himself as the other acts toward him. In our self-conscious experience we understand what he does or says. The possibility of this entering into his experience we have found in the cortex of the human brain. There the coördinations answering to an indefinite number of acts may be excited, and while holding each other in check enter into the neural process of adjustment which leads to the final overt conduct. If one pronounces and hears himself pronounce the word "table," he has aroused in himself the organized attitudes of his response to that object, in the same fashion as that in which he has aroused it in another. We commonly call such an aroused organized attitude an idea, and the ideas of what we are saying accompany all of our significant speech. If we may trust to the statement in one of St. Paul's epistles, some of the saints spoke with tongues which had no significance to them. They made sounds which called out no response in those that made them. The sounds were without meaning. Where a vocal gesture uttered by one individual leads to a certain response in another, we may call it a symbol of that act; where it arouses in the man who makes it the tendency to the same response, we may call it a significant symbol. These organized attitudes which we arouse in ourselves when we talk to others are, then, the ideas which we say are in our minds, and in so far as they arouse the same attitudes in others, they are in their minds, in so far as they are self-conscious in the sense in which I have used that term. But it is not necessary that we should talk to another to have these ideas. We can talk to ourselves, and this we do in the inner forum of what we call thought. We are in possession of selves just in so far as we can and do take the attitudes of others toward ourselves and respond to those attitudes. We approve of ourselves and condemn ourselves. We pat ourselves upon the back and in blind fury attack ourselves. We assume the generalized attitude of the group, in the censor that stands at the door of our imagery and inner conversations, and in the affirmation of the laws and axioms of the universe of discourse. *Quod semper, quod ubique*. Our thinking is an inner conversation in which we may be taking the rôles of specific acquaintances over against ourselves, but usually it is with what I have termed the "generalized other" that we converse, and so attain to the levels of abstract thinking, and that impersonality, that so-called objectivity that we cherish. In this fashion, I conceive, have selves arisen in human behavior and with the selves their minds. It is an interesting study, that of the manner in which the self and its mind arises in every child, and the indications of the corresponding manner in which it arose in primitive man. I cannot enter into a discussion of this. I do wish, however, to refer to some of the implications of this conception of the self for the theory of social control.

I wish to recur to the position, taken earlier in this paper, that, if we recognize that experience is a process continually passing into the future, objects exist in nature as the patterns of our actions. If we reduce the world to a fictitious instantaneous present, all objects fall to pieces. There is no reason to be found, except in an equally fictitious mind, why any lines should be drawn about any group of physical particles, constituting them objects. However, no such knife-edge present exists. Even in the so-called specious present there is a passage, in which there is succession, and both past and future are there, and the present is only that section in which, from the standpoint of action, both are involved. When we take this passage of nature seriously, we see that the object of perception is the existent future of the act. The food is what the animal will eat, and his refuge is the burrow where he will escape from his pursuer. Of course the future is, as future, contingent. He may not escape, but in nature it exists there as the counterpart of his act. So far as there are fixed relations there, they are of the past, and the object involves both, but the form that it has arises from the ongoing act. Evolutionary biology, in so far as it is not mere physics and chemistry, proceeds perhaps unwittingly upon this assumption, and so does social science in so far as it is not static. Its objects are in terms of the habitat, the environment. They are fashioned by reactions. I am merely affirming the existence of these objects, affirming them as existent in a passing universe answering to acts.

In so far as there are social acts, there are social objects, and I take it that social control is bringing the act of the individual into relation with this social object. With the control of the object over the act, we are abundantly familiar. Just because the object is the form of the act, in this character it controls the expression of the act. The vision of the distant object is not only the stimulus to movement toward it. It is also, in its changing distance values, a continual control of the act of approach. The contours of the object determine the organization of the act in its seizure, but in this case the whole act is in the individual and the object is in his field of experience. Barring a breakdown in the structure or function, the very existence of the object insures its control of the act. In the social act, however, the act is distributed among a number of individuals. While there is or may be an object answering to each part of the act, existing in the experience of each individual, in the case of societies dependent upon physiological differentiation the whole object does not exist in the experience of any individual. The control may be exercised through the survival of those physiological differentiations that still carry out the life-process involved in the complex act. No complication of the act which did not mediate this could survive. Or we may take refuge in a controlling factor in the act, as does Bergson, but this is not the situation that interests us. The human societies in which we are interested are societies of selves. The human individual is a self only in so far as he takes the attitude of another toward himself. In so far as this attitude is that of a number of others, and in so far as he can assume the organized attitudes of a number that are coöperating in a common activity, he takes the attitudes of the group toward himself, and in taking this or these attitudes he is defining the object of the group, that which defines and controls the response. Social control, then, will depend upon the degree to which the individual does assume the attitudes of those in the group who are involved with him in his social activities. In the illustration already used, the man who buys controls his purchase from the standpoint of a value in the object that exists for him only in so far as he takes the attitude of a seller as well as a buyer. Value exists as an object only for individuals within whose acts in exchange are present those attitudes which belong to the acts of the others who are essential to the exchange.

The act of exchange becomes very complicated; the degree to which all the essential acts involved in it enter into the acts of all those engaged therein varies enormously, and the control which the object, i.e., the value, exercises over the acts varies proportionately. The Marxian theory of state ownership of capital, i.e., of exclusive state production, is a striking illustration of the breakdown of such control. The social object, successful economic production, as presented in this theory, fails to assume the attitudes of individual initiative which successful economic production implies. Democratic government, on the theory of action through universal interest in the issues of a campaign, breaks down as a control, and surrenders the government largely to the political machine, whose object more nearly answers to the attitudes of the voters and the non-voters.

Social control depends, then, upon the degree to which the individuals in society are able to assume the attitudes of the others who are involved with them in common endeavor. For the social object will always answer to the act developing itself in self-consciousness. Besides property, all of the institutions are such objects, and serve to control individuals who find in them the organization of their own social responses.

The individual does not, of course, assume the attitudes of the numberless others who are in one way or another implicated in his social conduct, except in so far as the attitudes of others are uniform under like circumstances. One assumes, as I have said, the attitudes of generalized others. But even with this advantage of the universal over the multiplicity of its numberless instances, the number of different responses that enter into our social conduct seems to defy any capacity of any individual to assume the rôles which would be essential to define our social objects. And yet, though modern life has become indefinitely more complex than it was in earlier periods of human history, it is far easier for the modern man than for his predecessor to put himself in the place of those who contribute to his necessities, who share with him the functions of government, or join with him in determining prices. It is not the number of participants, or even the number of different functions, that is of primary importance. The important question is whether these various forms of activities belong so naturally to the member of a human society that, in taking the rôle of another, his activities are found to belong to one's own nature. As long as the complexities of human society do not exceed those of the central nervous system, the problem of an adequate social object, which is identical with that of an adequate self-consciousness, is not that of becoming acquainted with the indefinite number of acts that are involved in social behavior, but that of so overcoming the distances in space and time, and the barriers of language and convention and social status, that we can converse with ourselves in the rôles of those who are involved with us in the common undertaking of life. A journalism that is insatiably curious about the human attitudes of all of us is the sign of the times. The other curiosities as to the conditions under which other people live, and work, and fight each other, and love each other, follow from the fundamental curiosity which is the passion of self-consciousness. We must be others if we are to be ourselves. The modern realistic novel has done more than technical education in fashioning the social object that spells social control. If we can bring people together so that they can enter into each other's lives, they will inevitably have a common object, which will control their common conduct.

The task, however, is enormous enough, for it involves not simply breaking down passive barriers such as those of distance in space and time and vernacular, but those fixed attitudes of custom and status in which our selves are imbedded. Any self is a social self, but it is restricted to the group whose rôles it assumes, and it will never abandon this self until it finds itself entering into the larger society and maintaining itself there. The whole history of warfare between societies and within societies shows how much more readily and with how much greater emotional thrill we realize our selves in opposition to common enemies than in collaboration with them. All over Europe, and more specifically at Geneva, we see nationals with great distrust and constant rebounds trying to put themselves in each other's places and still preserve the selves that have existed upon enmities, that they may reach the common ground where they may avoid the horror of war, and meliorate unendurable economic conditions. A Dawes Plan is such a social object, coming painfully into existence, that may control the conflicting interests of hostile communities, but only if each can in some degree put himself in the other's place in operating it. The World Court and the League of Nations are other such social objects that sketch out common plans of action if there are national selves that can realize themselves in the collaborating attitudes of others.

INDEX

ABSOLUTE Idealism, 161.
Alexander, S., 43, 44, 177.
Aristotle, 8, 35, 38, 89, 102, 103.
Augustine, 89.

BACON, F., 104.
Bergson, H., 21, 22, 26, 161, 163-164, 179, 180, 192.
Berkeley, 107, 134.
Bohr, G., 94.
Bohr atom, 61, 153.
Brahe, T., 114.
Bridgman, P. W., 147, 150.
Broglie, L. de, 13, 17, 141.

CAUSATION, defined, 33.
Cerebrum, mechanism of arousing response to physical thing in the organism, 126-133, 135-139, 182-184.
Cognition, as reconstructive, 3, 18, 22, 107-118, 140; differentiated from consciousness, 4-5; belongs only to selves, 178, 184.
Communication, conveyance of meaning, 83, 86, 87.
Consciousness, as meaning and ideation, 4, 68-90; of the self, 184-190, 192-195.

DAWES plan, 195.
Democritus, 38, 103.
Descartes, 98, 102, 103, 120, 138.
Dewey, J., 18, 115.
Du Bois-Reymond, E., 152.
Durations, as sliding presents, 28.

EDDINGTON, A. S., 3, 10, 46, 55, 57, 94.
Einstein, A., 21, 26, 40, 41, 51, 54, 56, 58, 64, 78, 82, 93, 94, 100, 104, 109, 110, 113, 157.
Emergence, does not follow from the past, 2; in Whitehead's philosophy, 10; in the present, 11; task of philosophy, 14, 42; as incompletely determined, 15-16; as conditioning the past, 18-19, 23; as conferring characters on the world, 35-36, 47, 50, 65-67; defined, 69.
Empathy, 137.
Energy, essential feature of the doctrine, 34; as nature of the physical thing, 146-147; see "Relativity, doctrine of."
Environment, relation to the organism, 4, 35-36, 42, 128, 165-195.
Epistemology, problem of, 68; of the scientist, 93, 95-96, 98-106, 140, 151; relation to perceptual experience, 107-111, 140-160; and experience, 115.
Euclidean Geometry, 142.
Euclidean space, 60, 149, 152, 159.
Event, defined, 21; uniqueness of the, 33; distinguished from things, 36, 144; exhaustive account of impossible, 38; cannot be a perceptual object, 111.
Evolution, general term covering emergence, 50; see "Emergence."

FARADAY, M., 59.
Fitzgerald contraction, 54.
Froebel, 186.
Future, denied existence, 1; see "Past," and "Present."

GALILEAN dynamics, 50.
Gaussian coördinates, 158.
General theory of relativity, 64, 157, 158, 160; see "Relativity, doctrine of."

HUME, 14, 134.

IDEA, nature of, 87; see "Consciousness, as meaning and ideation."
Induction, basis of rationality in the universe, 11-12.
Inference, operation in reflection, 68.

JAMES, Wm., 161.
Jeans, J., 3, 12, 21, 46.

KANT, 12, 14, 52, 134.
Kantian hypothesis, 46.
Kelvin, 109, 153.
Kinaesthetic imagery, 137.

LAPLACEAN hypothesis, 46.
Larmor, 45, 55, 109, 155.
League of Nations, 195.
Leibniz, 164.
Lipps, T., 123.
Locke, 126, 130, 134.
Lorentz, H. A., 40, 45, 54, 55, 58, 104, 109, 155.
Lovejoy, A. O., 149.

MACH, E., 94.
Marxian social theory, 192.
Matter, as the nature of things, 122; see "Physical thing."
Maxwell, J. C., 40, 45, 55, 56, 57, 109, 143, 155, 156.
Memory, refers to the conditioning phase of the passing present, 28-31.
Meyerson, E., 23, 102.
Michelson-Morley experiment, 40, 55, 56, 97, 104, 143, 156.
Millikan, R. A., 106, 153.
Mind, locus of past and future, 24; field of, 25, 80-81, 82; a natural development, 84-85, 172-173; belongs only to selves, 178, 184.
Minkowski, H., 94.
Minkowski space-time, 2, 9, 13, 58, 78, 82, 98, 113, 145, 153, 155, 162.
Morgan, L., 43.

NEWTON, 26, 41, 45, 65, 110, 123, 133, 137.
Newtonian world, 37, 40, 41, 42, 46, 53, 55, 62, 64, 93, 98, 103, 104, 109, 113, 120, 123, 138, 147, 148, 150, 152, 159.

ORGANISM, relation to the environment, 24-25, 33, 36, 68-90, 107-118, 128, 165-195; as process, 34, 38, 65; as social, 49, 165, 178; as physical thing, 119-120, 138.
Ostwald, W., 43, 147.

PARMENIDEAN Reality, 1, 38, 98, 102.
Passage, a temporal progress, 13-14; conditioning events, 16-19, 33, 77, 79, 85, 88, 96, 97; an abstraction, 21, 23; see "Present."
Past, denied existence, 1; revocable and irrevocable, 2-3, 13, 16, 26, 30; as viewed by the historian, 3, 8; in relation to the organism, 5-9, 88; as reinterpretation in present, 10, 12, 22, 27, 29, 76; conditioned by and conditioning the emergent,

15, 17-19, 25, 64; producing reality, 26; in memory, 28-31; how inadequate, 31; function in experience, 48.
Physical thing, perception of, 120, 141-160, 169-170; how related to the organism, 121-133; primary and secondary qualities of, 133, 137; as resistant to the organism, 134-139; as social, 169.
Planck, M., 17, 94.
Plato, 89, 104, 164.
Poincaré, H., 146.
Prepotent responses, 127-130.
Present, as becoming and disappearing, 1, 28; as conceived by the scientist, 9, 11; referent to the emergent, 23; temporal spread, 23-24, 90; as containing all implications and values which lie beyond it, 25, 27-28, 32, 36, 173-174, 190; social nature of, 47, 63; social character of, as a standpoint, 51, 52.
Probability, 33.
Ptolemaic system, 171.

QUANTA, 100, 104, 106.

REALITY, exists in a present, 1; transcends the present, 11; reference reversed, 60.
Relativity, paradoxes of, 12; expressed in organisms, 38; doctrine of, 39-46, 50-51, 52-67, 78, 79, 93, 95, 98-100, 104, 144-146, 153, 156-157.
Riemannian Geometry, 157, 158.
Rousseau, 52.
Russell, B., 82, 135.
Rutherford, E., 94, 106, 153.

SCHROEDER, 17, 94.
Science, physical vs. biological, 35; theories of, dependent upon perceptual findings, 61.
Social, nature of the present, 47, 63; organism as, 49; nature of the present as a standpoint, 51, 52; nature of thought, 62-63; science as a perspective, 165-195; act defined, 180-182.
Sommerfeld, A., 94.
Space-time, see "Minkowski space-time."
Special principle of relativity, 64, 157, 160.
Spinoza, 164.
St. Paul, 89, 189.

TENSOR Mathematics, 158.
Time, as passage without becoming, 19; relation to passage, 20; see "Relativity, doctrine of" and "Minkowski space-time."
Truth, test of, 68.

VITAL force, 35.
Visual experience, "reality" of, 106-118, 120.

WEYL, H., 21, 94.
Whitehead, A. N., 1, 10, 12, 19, 20, 23, 43, 49, 56, 78, 93, 94, 98, 100, 121, 143, 148, 149, 156, 162-164, 171.
Wordsworth, 186.
World Court, 195.

DATE DUE
